TEDDY FERRARA

TEDDY FERRARA

Christopher
Shinn

THEATRE COMMUNICATIONS GROUP   NEW YORK   2013

The publication of *Teddy Ferrara*, by Christopher Shinn, through TCG's Book Program, is made possible in part by the New York State Council on the Arts with the support of Governor Andrew Cuomo and the New York State Legislature.

TCG books are exclusively distributed to the book trade by Consortium Book Sales and Distribution.

LIBRARY OF CONGRESS CATALOGING-IN-PUBLICATION DATA

Shinn, Christopher.
Teddy Ferrara / Christopher Shinn.
pages cm
ISBN 978-1-55936-450-8 (pbk.)
1. Gay students—Drama. I. Title.
PS3569.H498T43   2014
813'.54—dc23   2013026229

Book design and composition by Lisa Govan
Cover photograph by Andreas Ackerup / Link Image / Gallery Stock
Cover design by Mark Melnick

First Edition, November 2013

For Max

TEDDY FERRARA

Teddy Ferrara received its world premiere at Goodman Theatre (Robert Falls, Artistic Director; Roche Schulfer, Executive Director) in Chicago on February 11, 2013. It was directed by Evan Cabnet; set design was by Lee Savage, costume design was by Jenny Mannis, lighting design was by Keith Parham, sound design was by Richard Woodbury; the production stage manager was Dana M. Nestrick and the dramaturg was Tanya Palmer. The cast was:

GABE	Liam Benzvi
DREW	Adam Poss
NICKY	Rashaad Hall
TEDDY	Ryan Heindl
TIM	Josh Salt
JENNY	Paloma Nozicka
PRESIDENT	Patrick Clear
PROVOST	Janet Ulrich Brooks
ELLEN	Kelli Simpkins
JAQ	Jax Jackson
JAY	Christopher Imbrosciano
CAMPUS POLICE	Dev Kennedy and Fawzia Mirza

The time is now.

The place is on and nearby the campus of a large state university in the Northeast.

CHARACTERS

GABE, twenty-one

DREW, twenty-one

NICKY, twenty

TEDDY, eighteen

TIM, twenty-one

JENNY, twenty-one

PRESIDENT, sixties

PROVOST, fifties

ELLEN, forties

JAQ, twenty-four

JAY, twenty-one

CAMPUS POLICE, thirties

NOTES

The design should be simple in order to maximize speed of storytelling.

Interval between 3.7 and 4.1.

Love: what the heart aches for.

—J. M. Coetzee,
Diary of a Bad Year

1.1

Drew enters.

DREW: Need help?

GABE: Hey!

DREW: Jesus. Sure this wasn't the meeting of the Dessert Club?

GABE: I said refreshments in the fliers. I thought more people might come if we had cupcakes.

DREW: So either no one came, or you got a lot of cupcakes.

GABE: No one had any! Maybe gay guys don't want to be fat?

DREW: But dykes don't care about that.

GABE: Drew!

DREW: Um, it's true—lesbians are not as body-obsessed as gay dudes.

GABE: Well, we're still not really attracting lesbians. I opened the box and everyone just stared!

DREW: If I'd been here I would have had one.

GABE: But you weren't.

DREW: That is true, I was not! Mm, this is good. Too sweet— which is good.

GABE: Some people had Diet Coke. It's so hard to get people interested in this group!

DREW: Queer students want to spend their time being queer, not in a Queer Students group.

GABE: Why is it so hard to build a community? It's so frustrating to me—

DREW: I'm telling you—Friday's the deadline to declare—if you really want to make an impact—

GABE: Drew, I am not going to be Student Assembly President!

DREW: You would win.

GABE: I'm not that kind of—big personality.

DREW: Yes you are! —Are you not doing it because you think Tim would be mad at you?

GABE: Why would Tim be mad? He's not running for reelection.

DREW: I don't understand, you want to make a difference so badly— why won't you do it?

GABE: God! A week of dating and you're already telling me what to do!

DREW: Hey, that's mean!

GABE: Kidding! Kidding . . .

(They kiss.)

DREW: And it's a week and a half—*jerk*—

(Teddy enters.)

TEDDY: Is this the Queer Students meeting?

DREW: It's over.

GABE: It was three to four—but I can fill you in—what's your name?

TEDDY: Ted Ferrara—Teddy—Ted—

GABE: Ted Ferrara. I'll add you on Facebook—all we did today was talk about who we are, brainstorm ideas—I'll message you about it later. We're sponsoring a dance party Thursday, if you can come to that—and we meet here every Tuesday, three to four.

TEDDY: I thought it was four.

GABE: Nothing much happens at the first meeting. Hopefully you can come to the dance party. It's just off campus, at The Lair, eighteen to get in—all the info's on our website.

TEDDY: Okay.

(Teddy exits.)

DREW: What a weirdo.

GABE: He was a little awkward . . .

DREW: Um: weirdo.

GABE: He looks like a freshman. I was a *mess* my first year—until I met Tim—

DREW: Are you in love with Tim?

GABE: Am I in love with Tim? What's that supposed to mean?

DREW: He's hot, you're always talking about him—

GABE: He's my best friend. And he's straight.

DREW: You can't be in love with a straight guy? You're attracted to men—he's a man.

GABE: Well. No, I'm not in love with Tim. —I should have offered him a cupcake.

DREW: He wouldn't have taken it. Let's go somewhere and make out.

GABE: What am I going to do with all these?

(Drew kisses Gabe.)

Don't you have to do newspaper stuff?

DREW: Yes, but I want to make out.

GABE: Ha—stop.

DREW: Come over for a little—

GABE: I thought you had to work all day because you have that big story coming out—

DREW: Okay, so come to my office—

GABE: I have work to do—

DREW: No you don't—

GABE: I have a paper for my Political Anthropology class—

DREW: God! So unromantic—

GABE: I think another group has this room at 4:30—so we should—

DREW: It's 4:03! We could come twice in that time!

GABE: Have sex in a classroom? Are you *insane*?

DREW: I was just kidding. God, you take everything so seriously!

GABE: Oh. Well—I'm a serious person.

DREW: Which is why you should run for President. And *before* you yell at me for saying that—wanna come over tonight? I'd like to make you dinner. And you could stay the night . . .

GABE: Like . . . ?

DREW: Like—I'll cook dinner. And you'll sleep over for the first time.

(Pause.)

What?

GABE: Nothing—

DREW: You seem, like, scared suddenly.

GABE: No—

DREW: Why are you scared?

GABE: I'm not! I'm just thinking.

DREW: About?

GABE: No, I just—in my head you had that big story so—I just assumed you'd be working—

DREW: I have time. Come over at nine.

GABE: . . . Okay.

DREW: You're scared for some reason. What the fuck.

GABE: I'm not. I'm *not*.

(Teddy enters.)

TEDDY: Sorry—I just—it's under Ted Ferrara.

GABE: Oh—right.

TEDDY: I couldn't remember if I—said Teddy or Ted—

GABE: You said both but—Ted—yeah—I'll find you.

TEDDY: Sorry—

DREW *(Going)*: I gotta run—see you tonight!

(Drew exits. Pause.)

GABE: Want a cupcake?

TEDDY: Sure.

GABE: You can have more to—give to your roommate or—

TEDDY: Oh—um . . .

GABE: You don't have to. I just have a lot extra. So are you a freshman?

TEDDY: Yeah.

GABE: So a couple weeks—how's it going?

TEDDY: It's good . . .

GABE: It's a big school, it can be a tough transition. Are you from nearby?

TEDDY: Forty-five minutes . . .

GABE: Yeah. So not too far. I had a kind of hard time adjusting at first . . .

TEDDY: I like it so far . . .

GABE: I also did a double major, Political Science and English—*and* worked. Do you work?

TEDDY: I'm—I do computer programming—on my own, I make money doing that . . .

GABE: Oh wow, that's cool. Yeah—a lot of kids don't work, a lot of them are rich—

TEDDY: That guy is, you can tell.

GABE: Oh—yeah—I got a big fellowship over the summer, this'll be the first year I haven't had to work. Actually have some free time my senior year! *And* I finally got a single!

TEDDY: Yeah . . . My roommate is kind of weird.

GABE: He is?

TEDDY: I think he's freaked out I'm gay a little.

(Pause.)

GABE: What did he—did he say or do something specific?

TEDDY: I don't know . . . not really. I don't know. He's okay.

(Pause.)

GABE: Is he cute at least?

TEDDY: Ha. I don't know . . .

GABE: Well . . . hopefully you can come to the dance party Thursday.

TEDDY: Yeah.

GABE: And I'll message you. Ted Ferrara.

(Teddy smiles and exits.)

1.2

President enters.

PRESIDENT: They're pissed off? By the way, when did they become the Social Justice Committee?

PROVOST: At the final meeting last semester.

PRESIDENT: What was wrong with Diversity Committee?

PROVOST: They felt the name was too ocular.

PRESIDENT: In English.

PROVOST: Just because you see a lot of people of color and women and gays in a room—it doesn't necessarily mean anything. What matters are the values they're advocating for.

PRESIDENT: Right. So is my good friend Ellen leading the charge?

PROVOST: I know you think she doesn't like you—

PRESIDENT: She might like me, but she also wants to cut my balls off. Not mutually exclusive.

PROVOST: She's—well, did you get a chance to look at the working group report?

PRESIDENT: I saw how long it was and decided to contemplate suicide instead.

PROVOST: Well—

PRESIDENT: Are there things we can implement right away?

PROVOST: That's the issue. They feel we've moved too slowly—it got pretty heated at the last—

PRESIDENT: So what can we give them quickly?

PROVOST: Well, they were crafty—they're asking for big things—

PRESIDENT: So we can't get off the hook by giving them small things. I can't believe I thought I was getting out of politics by taking this job. I wasn't naive—but the extent of it!

PROVOST: Well—since you bring it up—

PRESIDENT: What—the rumors I'm going to run for Senate?

PROVOST: Well—let me get to the heart of things.

PRESIDENT: The working group report isn't the heart of things?

PROVOST: No. The reason I wanted to talk to you so urgently is— Ellen has heard a rumor. Kevin Gillman—the student who committed suicide last year—

PRESIDENT: Of course—

PROVOST: Well, the rumor is that the *Daily* is about to publish a story saying—that he was gay. The implication being that the climate at the university—led to, or contributed to, his suicide.

PRESIDENT: That kid had a psychotic break. He was on LSD.

PROVOST: Right—

PRESIDENT: He was giggling as he leapt off the balcony. There were witnesses all over the library.

PROVOST: I don't know the details of the story or what the evidence is—but that's the rumor.

PRESIDENT: And what? They're ready to turn this into a big—

PROVOST: I think it's in our interest to get out in front of it. Because of the rumors you might run for the Senate again—I think they think the press will pay more attention to what's happening at the school—so they could potentially turn this into a much bigger—

PRESIDENT: What do you think they want? I mean what's the thing they're not expecting us to give them that we actually could give them without, you know—creating a new bureaucracy.

PROVOST: You should read the report.

PRESIDENT: You're so ominous. Is it that out there?

PROVOST: What they want would mean a fundamental shift in the university culture.

PRESIDENT: What's one example.

PROVOST: Requiring diversity on syllabi.

PRESIDENT: *Requiring?*

PROVOST: All syllabi would be screened by the Provost's office to ensure that writers from minority groups were included in the course readings.

PRESIDENT: You're kidding. What about academic freedom?

PROVOST: Many of them see true academic freedom as necessitating diversity. There are various levels of support for the idea but even on the milder spectrum—they want the university to put real pressure on professors to have diverse syllabi.

PRESIDENT: What else?

PROVOST: Gender-neutral bathrooms.

PRESIDENT: I thought we had those.

PROVOST: We have some. They want them in the same proportion as men's and women's.

PRESIDENT: Like—literally wherever we have two bathrooms—

PROVOST: There would be a third option for transgender and gender-variant students.

PRESIDENT: How many transgender students do we have?

PROVOST: There's controversy about the actual number but— probably a few hundred—

PRESIDENT: Out of forty thousand—and they don't see the absurdity—just in terms of cost alone—

PROVOST: They don't see their task as having anything to do with practical—

PRESIDENT: But isn't the point of being transgender that you— want to be a specific gender?

PROVOST: The argument is that gender-questioning and transgender students often don't feel comfortable or safe in either of the—

PRESIDENT: Okay. So what you're saying is this is not gonna be an easy—I got it.

PROVOST: I suggest we have a lunch tomorrow—invite Ellen and some students from this population—and begin a dialogue. So if that article comes out we can say—

PRESIDENT: We've already been—smart. Let's do it. *(Going)* Want to run my Senate campaign?

1.3

TIM *(On phone)*: Dude, she is so hot. Thank God it's still warm—
her *legs*. No, she's standing for some reason. I think she's eating a knish. She's hot eating a knish. That is crazy.

No—she messaged me to ask what she missed in class and I told her, and she wrote back, "Why did you take Twentieth-Century Fiction?" And I wrote, "The books are shorter than older books." And she wrote, "Right, more time to look at porn."

Dude—I'm like a gentle breeze away from a boner. Why do I have a girlfriend again? Think Jenny would mind if I cheated on her just once—

(Gabe enters on phone.)

GABE: You are such a pig—
TIM: Check her out—
GABE: Hang up!

(They hang up their phones.)

TIM: See?

GABE: Fine, she has nice legs!

TIM: Since when do they have knish here—

GABE: So: I'm this weird mix of excited and upset!

TIM: Yeah, what's up?

GABE: Well, the excited part—I'm having lunch with the President tomorrow.

TIM: Of the United States?

GABE: No! The school.

TIM: What's the reason?

GABE: I think he wants to talk about LGBT issues. It's a really small group—

TIM: That's awesome. Can I give you a tip? His mind wanders. It seems like he's not paying attention—but he is. He's just, like, super curious and tangential. Don't get nervous. Just keep talking, he's totally hearing you. Also, he really likes people who speak their mind.

GABE: Cool, thanks.

TIM: What are you upset about?

GABE: So I was supposed to meet Drew at nine for dinner.

TIM: Uh-huh?

GABE: The President's office called at five and—I got excited. It's a really big opportunity. And I started, like, daydreaming—what if he runs for the Senate, I'm graduating in the spring, could I work for his campaign, could I work in his Senate office—I didn't get my work done, it was 6:30, and I just—I felt like it would be better if I saw Drew another time. I need to write this paper and I wanted time to mentally prepare for tomorrow—

TIM: Of course!

GABE: So I texted him and asked if we could get together tomorrow instead—I explained everything and I just said Wednesday would be nicer because the lunch will be over—

TIM: Yeah?

GABE: He didn't text me back. And he is *always* on his phone for newspaper stuff—he always texts back. So I texted again. Nothing. So then I called, left a message. *Then* he texted me.

(Shows Tim his phone.)

TIM: Whoa. Jumping to conclusions a little!

GABE: I know! "Scared of intimacy," I mean—

TIM: That is crazy. You have a huge day tomorrow!

GABE: So I texted him back and told him I could see him any time this week, just not tonight—

TIM: What did he say?

GABE: Nothing yet.

TIM: I need to meet this dude so I can decide if you're allowed to let him ruin our senior year.

GABE: I guess I'll just see how he responds . . . Anyway—you meeting Jenny now?

TIM: Yes but I have a cheating fantasy taking root.

GABE: Not *really* though.

TIM: Oh, she's leaving. Finished her knish. Am I gonna let her go? I am—

GABE: You really want to cheat on Jenny?

TIM: No . . . But—we're not gonna get married, are we? We're twenty-one.

GABE: But you really love her . . .

TIM: Yeah . . . I mean I *think* I love her—but do I *really*?

GABE: Yes! You've been going out since the beginning of freshman year!

TIM: I don't know why I'm having these thoughts suddenly—

GABE: Part of me thinks I'm falling in love with Drew.

TIM: After one week?

GABE: Yeah—

(Jenny enters.)

JENNY: Hey! Hi, Gabe, I didn't you were gonna be here—

TIM: You're early!

JENNY: Just five minutes. There was literally nothing to do in the admissions office today—

GABE: So you guys are getting some food—

TIM: We are! Wanna come?

GABE: I would, but I have stuff to do, I'm just gonna grab something—

TIM: Gabe has boyfriend problems.

GABE: I do, sort of—

JENNY: He's a boyfriend already? That's great!

GABE: Maybe—we'll see—

TIM: We're going to get pizza, isn't that right?

JENNY: Is that what we're getting?

TIM: I thought that's we decided upon after considering the many delicious options.

GABE: Before you go—I actually had one more thing to ask you—

TIM: Jesus! You're falling apart!

GABE: Shut up. You can answer, too, Jenny. Drew—had this idea that I should run for Student Assembly President. At first I was like, No, that's not really my personality—but then—I don't know, part of me started to think—I do want to work in politics—maybe I should do it—but—I don't know, do you think I would actually like it? *If* I won of course—

JENNY: You'd love it! It's just like a bigger version of what you do with the Queer Students—

TIM: I mean—yeah—I think you'd like it—for sure.

GABE: Really?

TIM: The only thing to think about is how important it is to you to have fun this year. It is a lot of—meetings and—you definitely wouldn't have as much time to fart around—

GABE: But you had—free time last year, we hung out a lot—

TIM: True, but you'd be getting used to it for a while since you've never—it would be a lot. I know you were psyched not to have to work this year . . .

JENNY: You should totally do it. Like you said, it's what you want to do.

GABE: And you liked it, I mean—but you didn't want to do it again—

TIM: I wanted to have fun senior year. But—yeah, you know—interesting issues come up, you get a lot of face time with important people in the administration, it's great on your résumé—you just have to decide how important free time is to you.

GABE: Right. But it's not like I wouldn't have *any* free time—

TIM: Just make sure you really want to do it and it's not just about that this guy wants you to.

GABE: No—it's my own . . .

JENNY: I want to meet him. We should all go out!

TIM: Yeah, let's get drinks soon—before you dump his ass!

GABE: Ha. Maybe we could do it before the dance party—if you guys are coming. He's not.

TIM: He's *not*?

GABE: He doesn't like gay clubs—

TIM: I don't know, are we going?—

JENNY: Aren't you working Friday morning?

TIM: No, I switched shifts with someone, so I'm doing Saturday and Sunday brunch now.

JENNY: Oh. Well—let's say drinks before, and if we can go to the dance party—

GABE: Cool, I'll see what he says—if he's ever in touch again. Anyway—thanks for meeting up!

TIM: Later!

JENNY: Bye, Gabe!

(They go. Teddy approaches Gabe.)

GABE: Oh—hey!

TEDDY: Hi—

GABE: I haven't added you yet—sorry. Turned out to be a busy day.

TEDDY: It's okay.

GABE: I'll do it later tonight—

TEDDY: Was that your boyfriend?

GABE: No—that's my best friend.

TEDDY: I meant from before . . .

GABE: Oh—we're—figuring that out I guess!

TEDDY: How did you meet?

GABE: We just—we sort of knew each other from around, but we'd never really talked—I got back to school and I ran into him on my way to the library . . . and we just started talking.

TEDDY: What did you guys talk about?

GABE: There was an article in the *Daily* about the group I run—so we talked about that at first. He doesn't really like the idea of a Queer Student Group, he thinks it's too "segregated"—

TEDDY: I have a date tonight—

GABE: Oh yeah? Nice!

TEDDY: This guy I met on Manhunt.

GABE: Ahh.

TEDDY: I asked my roommate if I could have the room to myself from nine to eleven, so . . .

GABE: Is he—you said you thought he was freaked out that you were gay, right?

TEDDY: I don't know, he let me have it, so—I think he's pretty cool, just a little awkward . . .

GABE: Well—definitely—if you come to the dance party—you might meet people that way, too.

TEDDY: Yeah. We'll see how it goes . . .

GABE: Good luck—

TEDDY: Did you ever do that—Manhunt?

GABE: Um—you know, it's not really my thing—

TEDDY: Have you had lots of boyfriends?

GABE: I've dated but—that's one of the reasons for the group actually—to try to create a community of . . . It's really hard to meet people, even in this day and age—

TEDDY: Hopefully it'll go well tonight with this guy, so . . .

GABE: Yeah—well, I should get going—

TEDDY: Okay—

GABE: I'll message you later though!

(Gabe goes. Teddy takes out his phone, snaps a picture of himself.)

1.4

NICKY: What is he saying?

DREW: Sorry, just finishing . . .

NICKY: Does he admit he got scared—

DREW: Nope!

NICKY: That sucks.

DREW: The email is basically just him asking me to have drinks with his friends Thursday before the dance.

NICKY: Nothing about how he freaked out when you invited him over?

DREW: No! It's like he won't even acknowledge what I wrote. —Anyway. What's up?

NICKY: So . . . I thought more about the piece and—I just don't feel comfortable putting my name on it.

DREW: What are you talking about? We're about to go to press.

NICKY: I just keep coming back to—there has to be some other evidence Kevin was gay.

DREW: Nicky, we resolved this! When he told me freshman year that he thought he might be gay, he told me he had *never told anyone* and that he would probably *never act on it*.

NICKY: How could he not tell anyone else *ever*. It doesn't make—

DREW: He was incredibly private, and he didn't want to be gay!

NICKY: But you guys weren't in touch after freshman year. You really think he never—

DREW: In his mind, he was settled—he was not going to deal with that part of himself. Which is *why* he ditched me and why he never spoke to me again! —You saw his emails to me—

NICKY: But those just show that you guys were friends, there was nothing in them that—I really feel like I should go back and ask people who knew him if there was anything—

DREW: All they'll say is that he wasn't gay, because he *never told anyone*—why is this so hard to—

NICKY: I just—maybe if it wasn't that the anonymous source was also the editor of the paper—

DREW: But that's the only way this story can get told. I'm the only person who knows!

NICKY: But it is a conflict of interest, you have to admit that.

DREW: I've gotten media attention from other stories I've published, I don't *need* this to—

NICKY: If there's just one more piece of the puzzle that—

DREW: Nicky, *all over the country* kids are killing themselves because they're gay. Because *still* in this day and age it's not acceptable. Because *still* there is bullying, and hate, and prejudice. We *need* to tell this story. Go on Manhunt—how many closeted guys are on there? How many frat boys are getting blowjobs in the ninth-floor library bathroom—

NICKY: Well what I was thinking is—why not write a first-person piece? That solves the whole—

DREW: Because then the story becomes about me. It will seem like self-promotion.

NICKY: But it will have the same impact and it's up front. You're speaking honestly about—

DREW: People won't believe me. He was so hot. People will say I'm delusional.

NICKY: Drew—you're a really sexy guy—

DREW: You know what he looked like. He was like an Abercrombie & Fitch model.

NICKY: Well—I think it's also that . . . —You won't really tell me exactly what *happened* . . .

DREW: You mean that I won't go into all the details?

NICKY: Yeah. "Hooked up" can mean anything—if the point of the piece is that he's gay—

DREW: It's a piece about *all* his possible motives—why would you need every little—

NICKY: Come on—the point is to say that he was gay—

DREW: Hold on a second—are we done with the earlier discussion? Did I miss something?

NICKY: It just—it started to bug me. I respected at the time that you didn't want to go into too many details because it was still painful—but there's a difference between *sex* and just—

DREW: But are you saying now that if I tell you exactly what happened you'll be okay with putting your name on it?

NICKY: Well—depending on what happened . . .

DREW: Then it's okay that I'm the editor and I'm the single source for the—

NICKY: I—yeah. I just need *something* more—to believe that he was gay . . .

DREW: Nicky. It happened one time. After it happened, he'd pass me in the dorm like he didn't even know me. It was *incredibly* painful. And that's all I'm going to say.

NICKY: So—you'd rather not tell me more of what happened than have the article published—

DREW: Fine. I'll pull the article.

NICKY: Why—can't you write it as a—

DREW *(Gets text)*: Whoa.

NICKY: What?

DREW: Gabe is going to run for Student Assembly President. He just decided.

NICKY: Oh . . .

DREW: Imagine if we had a gay President. How awesome would that be!

(Pause.)

NICKY: All right—you can publish it with my name on it.

(Pause.)

DREW: You're sure? It's up to you.

NICKY: It's fine, I'm just being— *(Going)* I'll talk to you later.

DREW: Thank you!

1.5

TEDDY (*On computer, dressed, wearing ear buds, intermittently types as he speaks into his computer*): Nine. No, he's going to call me when he gets here. He's not a student, I have to sign him in. He's not here, I asked him if I could have the room from nine to eleven and he said yeah. Two hours seemed long enough but you never know, ha.

If he was *hot* . . . then I would definitely jerk off in his bed when he wasn't here. But he's not hot.

You want me to show you his dirty underwear? I just told you, he's not hot!

Slow down with the questions! One at a time. Jeez.

I am not leaving the camera on. Ha. No, you do *not* get to see that.

I have all these canker sores right now. What causes them, anyone know? Can I give a blowjob with canker sores? Hurts.

Why would he come in if he promised me the room? You're delusional, he's not gay.

You wanna see what he's getting? Yeah? You want a peek? Ha. All right . . .

(Teddy stands, starts to push down his pants. The phone rings.)

Shit—gotta go. Sorry. Later, studs!

(Teddy closes the computer, readies himself, and exits.)

1.6

GABE: Welcome to my luxurious single!

DREW: Yeah. There's a reason we've been hanging out at my place.

GABE: It took me three years to nab this. Look at the beautiful exposed cinderblock wall . . .

DREW: And this tiny bed. Don't you think they should give you bigger beds at *some point*?

GABE: You'd need bigger rooms.

DREW: There's room for a fifty-thousand-seat stadium. I think you've found your winning issue!

GABE: I highly doubt luxury dorms are in the university's long-term planning.

DREW: That's the benefit of having me as a boyfriend—if that's what we are.

(Pause.)

GABE: Right.

DREW: We really like each other, I thought.

GABE: I—yeah.

DREW: So why are you getting cold feet?

GABE *(Gets text)*: Sorry, just—
DREW: Jesus! What the fuck—
GABE: Tim wants to get a beer—I'll tell him no—
DREW: It can't wait till we're done talking?
GABE: It'll take two seconds.
DREW: It's up to you.

(Pause. Gabe texts.)

GABE: Okay. So. I just—I do want to apologize.
DREW: Sure you wouldn't rather just text me an apology?
GABE: Drew! I invited you over—
DREW: But you seem to prefer things to be at a distance, so—
GABE: I'm not scared of intimacy. But I did—hesitate when you asked me to come over earlier. And—I've thought about it and—I think you're right. —I did get scared in that moment.
DREW: Why?
GABE: I just—something about you cooking dinner and staying over . . .
DREW: It was a step.
GABE: Yeah.
DREW: And you don't want to take a step?
GABE: I do, I just . . .
DREW: Just . . . ?
    I've been really hurt in the past. That's something you need to know.
GABE: Who—hurt you?
DREW: I don't want to talk about it now.
GABE: Why not?
DREW: I don't feel safe.

(Pause.)

    If you're going to get scared and run—do it now. I can't go through that later on.
GABE: I mean . . . I can't say for sure where things will go with us—
DREW: I'm not asking you to marry me! I know things might not work out, just—if you know you're not really up to this—then let me go now.

(Pause.)

GABE: I think what happened was—this morning—you know, I woke up horny and—usually I jerk off to porn or—I think about someone I really want but could never have—

DREW: Tim?

GABE: No—no, someone—that I don't know, really, like a hot guy I see or—

DREW: You could have hot guys—

GABE: No, like, they're straight or—anyway, I started to—jerk off and—*you* came into my head. It's the first time—someone—that I fantasized to someone that I had actually been with.

(Pause.)

DREW: I don't understand, are you saying you don't want me in reality?

GABE: No—the opposite! I got—it freaked me out for some reason. I tried to put you out of my head and put other guys there and—you kept coming back, I couldn't—finally I just gave over to it—and I had this amazing orgasm, much more intense than usual and . . . I just *freaked*. It felt—so *real* now. Then I cleaned up and sort of put it out of my head and told myself it didn't mean anything—but then when you invited me to stay over . . .

DREW: It felt real again.

GABE: And when I got the call from the President's office . . .

DREW: You used that as an excuse.

(Pause. Gabe approaches Drew. He kisses him.)

Wait—

GABE: What?

DREW: Do you know what I want?

(Pause.)

GABE: You want . . . to be loved.

DREW: Yeah, but—more specifically . . .

GABE: Okay . . .
DREW: I want monogamy.
    Trust.
    No lies.
    No games.

(Pause.)

GABE: I understand.
    I want those things, too.

(Pause.)

I love you, Drew.
DREW: I love you, too.

(They kiss.)

1.7

TEDDY *(On his computer as before)*: No. Not in the mood. For those of you just coming in—I'm just looking to talk. Go jerk off to someone else's cam.

Yes. He came over. I don't kiss and tell, sorry.

No, not till after. If I'd noticed it before why would I—

Ugh, pay attention, people! I walked the guy out. Yes he was hot. When I came back to my room I noticed my roommate's webcam pointed at my bed. It's never been that direction before. So I checked his Facebook and Twitter—he posted that I was hooking up with a guy *and* said that he had just been watching us, remotely. Yeah, using his webcam on someone else's computer—

I'm not sure. Student code says "recorded"—I don't know if he recorded me, he probably just broadcast it—and I can tell from the angle that he probably couldn't see much—maybe just the edge of the bed—so I don't know if they can do anything . . .

Oh yeah—I don't know how many people saw but—all these people wrote on his Wall, like, "Ew," "How can you go back in there." I screengrabbed it. I have evidence!

Might talk to my RA or fill out a new-roommate-request form. I don't know yet. I have to think about it. I mean they probably won't even do anything about it . . .

I have the room till eleven at least, so I have an hour I guess . . . God, you guys are hungry for my cock tonight—

Ugh, *fine!* —Duh, I turned off his computer as soon as I saw his Facebook—

(He stands up and begins to touch himself over his clothes.)

Mm. Yeah . . . God, I guess I'm still fucking horny . . .

2.1

Alarm goes off.

GABE: Uhhhhnnnn!
DREW: Ha!
GABE: You seem awake . . .
DREW: I've been up for a while.
GABE: Why?
DREW: Couldn't sleep.
GABE: You've just been laying here? How long?
DREW: What else am I going to do?
GABE: Go out and get me breakfast?
DREW: Ha . . . No, I just watched you.
GABE: You watched me?
DREW: Watched you sleep. You're beautiful.

(*Pause.*)

GABE: Thanks.
   Why couldn't you sleep?
DREW: Probably this bed.

GABE: I know. It's a miracle we slept at all—

DREW: Did you have a bad dream?

GABE: A bad dream? . . .

DREW: Like twenty minutes ago you were moving around a lot. Just for a little bit.

GABE: Oh . . . I did have a dream . . . It wasn't bad though . . .

DREW: What was it?

GABE: It was a dream about Tim.

DREW: Of course.

GABE: What?

DREW: You're so obviously in love with him!

GABE: Stop saying that!—

DREW: What was the dream?

GABE: All I remember is—we went to the university bookstore together. And he wanted to buy me *The Scarlet Letter*—but I said I already had two copies.

    That's it.

DREW: Obvious.

GABE: What? I want to have sex with him?

DREW: The opposite. You're finally figuring out that he wants to have sex with you.

(Pause.)

GABE: I need to get some breakfast—want to come?

DREW: How many straight guys do you know whose best friend is gay?

GABE: We've gone camping alone together, we've slept next to each other for—if he wanted to try something—I don't even understand how that's your interpretation!

DREW: Well what's yours?

GABE: He—misses me a little. Since I started dating you. And he wants to give me something.

DREW: Give you what?

GABE: Something—I don't know. Something I—don't need?

DREW: *That's* my interpretation! He wants to give you something you already have—*me*. Sex!

GABE: Wait—how are you *The Scarlet*—

DREW: It's a book about sex!

GABE: No, that's—I think it's—we're both Political Science majors and English minors. It's going back to how we met freshman year, how we bonded over doing the same—

DREW: How many hundreds of books could your unconscious have chosen.

GABE: You're crazy.

DREW: Did you wake up with a boner?

GABE: I—always wake up with a boner. *(Gets text)* Funny. Tim.

DREW: Big surprise . . .

GABE: Wow—that's kind of weird . . .

DREW: What?

GABE: No, I'm—he just wanted to tell me he's decided to run for reelection after all.

DREW: Whoa—did he say why he changed his mind?

GABE: Just that he thought about it some more and he'd like to do it again. "Hope that's okay."

DREW: You really think that's the reason—

GABE: I gotta get this day started, get ready for this lunch. You want to have breakfast?

DREW: I have newspaper stuff. I like how you changed the subject.

GABE: We're all getting drinks tomorrow! I'm uncomfortable talking about him this way!

DREW: All right. But he's really acting out I think. I bet he tries to break us up.

GABE: According to you, he's going to break into my room tonight and try to rape me!

DREW: If that happens, make sure you record it.

GABE: Stop!

DREW: So am I seeing you later?

GABE: I have some dance party stuff to do tonight. Thought any more about coming?

DREW: You really have to ask me that?

GABE: Well maybe after a few drinks with Tim and Jenny you'll change your mind.

DREW: I'm a journalist. I should never be in a *club*. I should be alone in a dive-bar feeling suicidal.

GABE: Yeah well . . . I guess we'll see each other *for a little while* Thursday.

DREW: For drinks with Tim and his fake girlfriend. Before you go ghettoize yourself at the club.

GABE: You are such a brat.

DREW: You love me for it.

GABE: Kind of . . .

DREW: You know you do. All right. You look ready to go.

GABE: I am.

DREW: Can I stay here for a little bit? I could use a little more sleep . . .

GABE: Sure. Of course.

DREW: Thanks.

(They kiss.)

I love you.

GABE: I love you, too.

DREW: And don't forget to declare today. You're gonna get busy with Queer Students crap—

GABE: Well—now I'm not sure.

DREW: Why not?

GABE: If Tim's running—

DREW: We need you, Gabe. You have to run.

GABE: I feel like I need to talk to Tim about it—

DREW: Don't think about him—you want to do it, just do it. What time's your lunch today?

GABE: One-thirty.

DREW: Good luck. Let me know how it goes.

GABE: Okay, will do.

(Gabe goes. Drew takes out his phone.)

DREW: Hey. You up? You ready for the big day?

It should go online around 1:30. Can you make sure you're cleaned up later? I have a feeling the news is really gonna jump on this story. You should be ready to go on TV.

I don't know, I just wanted to share it with you. I thought he looked so sweet, sleeping like . . . I was just bored.

Okay. See you in the office in a little bit.

2.2

Gabe enters with tray.

TEDDY: Hey.

GABE: Oh—hey! I still haven't messaged you—

TEDDY: It's okay.

GABE: It was a—I have this big lunch today— Are you coming to the dance party tomorrow?

TEDDY: Um—

GABE: You don't have to dance. I know people feel like—I'm not a great dancer—

TEDDY: I have all these canker sores . . .

GABE: Well—hopefully you'll feel better and can come.

TEDDY: I think it's just stress, I'm developing this new computer program. I'm a programmer—

GABE: Oh yeah? Cool—

TEDDY: All night I'm programming, a lot of people are dependent on the work I do—

GABE: Right. Oh—how did your date go?

TEDDY: Good. We have another date, so. Wait, tomorrow—I'm seeing him tomorrow, so.

GABE: Bring him to the dance party! Anyone can come—

TEDDY: I have a lot of programming to do, I'm on a deadline. Because so many people are—

GABE: Actually—my friend's here so I have to run—

TEDDY: Okay—

GABE: But—I'll message you—

(Teddy exits.)

(Going to Tim) Hey—

TIM: That's not Drew, is it?

GABE: You think I would have sex with *that*?

TIM: I don't know what turns you on!

GABE: No—he's just this kid who missed the first Queer Students meeting. You're not eating?

TIM: I want to get a run in before class. What's up?

GABE: I just—I mean I got your text obviously—

TIM: Yeah—

GABE: So I just wanted to—you're not, like, mad at me, are you?

TIM: For what?

GABE: No, I—because you weren't going to run and then—I mean I don't have to run—

TIM: No! Do it!

GABE: I only did it because you weren't—

TIM: I got it into my head that I wanted more free time this year but—I thought about it some more and I just changed my mind.

GABE: Right . . .

TIM: But I'm not mad you decided to run—I think it's awesome. May the best man win!

GABE: Okay . . . That was—I just wanted to—

TIM: Cool. All right, I'm gonna go get my run in—

GABE: Cool—and I know we haven't really had a chance to hang out much—

TIM: Understandable—you're getting to know this dude—

GABE: Right—soon I hope. —Oh—Drew is good for Thursday night if you guys are still up for—

TIM: Oh! Yeah . . . I think so. I'll have to check, but—

GABE: Cool.

TIM: Later!

(Tim goes.)

2.3

PRESIDENT: Sorry I'm late—Homecoming stuff—did you know we invited the cast of *Beach Crew*—

PROVOST: I know—

PRESIDENT: We're paying these morons thirty-four thousand dollars! For what? To act out scenes from their reality show?

PROVOST: The students voted in an online poll—they wanted them—of all the options—

PRESIDENT: This is gonna be a thing—

PROVOST: I know—so in the room—

PRESIDENT: I got the names—Ellen, Gabe, Jay and Jaq—Ellen I know obviously—

PROVOST: Jay is in the wheelchair—really bright kid, deeply involved in university issues—

PRESIDENT: Why's he in a wheelchair, what's his—

PROVOST: As I recall, he has a bone disorder—I don't know the specific—

PRESIDENT: Just curious—now Jaq—that's a funny spelling, with a "q"—

PROVOST: Jaq used to be Jacqueline—Jaq is transgender—currently transitioning—

PRESIDENT: So she changed her name—

PROVOST: He's in the graduate program in Gender Studies, so he's close to Ellen—

PRESIDENT: Won some awards for her writing—

PROVOST: His writing—you should refer to the gender . . . the person—

PRESIDENT: Right. I always find that weird but—Jay wheelchair, Jaq is a *he*—

PROVOST: And Gabe runs the Queer Students group—

PRESIDENT: When did it stop being the LGBTQ—

PROVOST: I think two years ago—

PRESIDENT: You were supposed to say, "When?" so I could say, "When they ran of out of letters!"

PROVOST: Right—

PRESIDENT: Here we go!

2.4

President and Provost enter.

PRESIDENT: Hello, everyone, sorry I'm late!

ELLEN: We've learned to be patient.

PRESIDENT: I hope pizza's okay. I thought it'd be fun if we kept things casual. Even got a vegan one!

(Pizza is eaten throughout the following.)

As a way of getting us into the discussion—I had an experience at the mall the other day—I was standing in line to get a cinnamon bun—mistake number one—and there was this group of teenage boys behind me—and every other word was "faggot" or "fag"—

PROVOST: Dig in everyone—

PRESIDENT: It was unbelievable. Finally I turned to them and said, "Why do you guys use all these derogatory terms for gay people, why is that?" The kid who looked like the leader, the good-looking one, shrugged his shoulders, like he had no idea.

I said, "Come on, there has to be a reason!" Nothing. I turned around, got my—these seemed like decent kids—

ELLEN: They've been socialized to believe that heterosexuality is the ideal, and homosexuality—

PRESIDENT: Sure—but isn't it also—there weren't any girls there—they're hanging out together, trying to look good—they're probably scared they're a little gay! So that's a way of—

ELLEN: Might be part of it. But if that's all it was, they could just talk about girls all the time.

PRESIDENT: Well, they were doing that, too. And in pretty offensive ways actually. I kept hearing these—"hymen ripping"—one kid said "anal bleeding" in reference to a girl—

ELLEN: The link to me is violence—whether it's gay men or women, the language—

PRESIDENT: That's interesting—that reminds me of another—a friend of mine—this is a little graphic but I think it's so illustrative—he has a teenage daughter, fourteen I think—and she had her first sexual experience—with a boy her age, I don't think she knew him very well—typical first time—but—she recounted this to her mother afterwards because she was so traumatized—they're having intercourse and at the climactic moment—the boy—it was his first time, too, I believe—he, instead of finishing—in the way he's been—forgive me for being graphic, but he pulls out of her and ejaculates on her face!

PROVOST: Nice lunch conversation—

PRESIDENT: Well look, on the one hand it is a—but the point is, the reason, the girl was upset and started crying and the boy ended up saying that—he had seen that in pornography so many times, he thought that's what—sex was, that when the man is about to finish—that that's what he does, that's what women like! He was upset, too, he didn't mean to—but from the time he was a little kid he's been seeing this stuff online—now that was sort of a tangent because it doesn't have anything to do with gay, or queer, issues but—I mean if you're gay, or transgender, or—you're living in this world where there's a lot of crass, demeaning, violent—I mean look at what's happening at Yale, one of our great universities being investigated by the federal government for a pervasive culture of sexual harassment—so this stuff is on my mind, this link between sex and degradation in our culture right now. And so this lunch—I want to know what we can do to change, to try to begin to change, I can't do it all myself, the school can't do, can't magically—but the question is, what *can* we do to begin to try to change the culture here—so that the pervasiveness of violence, even just verbally or—violence and sex, sexual orientation—how can we create a culture where those things aren't so linked?

PROVOST: As we eat our pizza.

PRESIDENT: Yes. Don't be shy! That's the—I was trying to set a tone, so no one feels shy—

ELLEN: You did a very good job.

PRESIDENT: Thank you, Ellen!

JAQ: Well one thing I'd like to know is—are you running for the Senate?

PRESIDENT: Ha! Not the lead-off I was expecting. Well—why do you ask?

JAQ: If you do—what kind of commitment can queer people expect from you as a Senator?

PRESIDENT: You taping this? Ha. Gotta ask these days. Look—to be frank—as a Senator you have one vote, it's a relatively limited, who knows what the—what I can say is that things are changing rapidly in this area and I support those changes. Now you'll accuse me of dodging your question but—can I ask, are you self-identified as transgender?

JAQ: I consider myself transgender, yes.

PRESIDENT: Now, just so I—you consider yourself—both, or—just the one you—feel yourself to be?

JAQ: I am a man.

PRESIDENT: So both a man and transgender—see this is fascinating, because this is sort of the new thing—you look back even ten years and this wasn't on the radar—it's like going back twenty years and I don't think anyone would have thought you'd have so many gay characters on TV—so I think you see how fast the culture is moving—I mean—I forget the number, but I think we have very few students who self-identify as transgender—

JAQ: There are a lot more than just those who self-identify on a form—

TEDDY FERRARA

43

PRESIDENT: Oh, sure, I didn't mean to imply—

PROVOST: We started the Gender Identity Task Force in 2005 because we perceived that transgender students didn't feel comfortable being open—

JAQ: There's also a lot of people somewhere on the continuum who—

PRESIDENT: That's what I mean, you're sort of a pioneer but— probably this will be, in ten or twenty years—I remember from my days reading Freud—you know, he thought everybody sort of—not to get into it too much—but there's always been these Hollywood actors ending up getting arrested with transvestites, right—I mean if everybody is sort of bisexual and has an inner woman and an inner man—anyway—my point is—

ELLEN: You have a point?

PRESIDENT: Believe it or not—ha—my point is—our job, if we can, is to try to help these things along, because society is slow— it's conservative—and universities have traditionally—

ELLEN: No, exactly, I agree. It's interesting to hear you free-associate on these—

PRESIDENT: Guilty as charged—

ELLEN: But I know our time is limited—and I want to focus on very concrete steps we can take—not that we should need this meeting to accomplish anything that should start happening through the Social Justice Committee working with the Provost's office—

PRESIDENT: No, that's all still—

ELLEN: But what a committee can't do, even when writing a very strongly worded report, is convey the emotional immediacy of these issues. I have students who want to die.

(Pause.)

PRESIDENT: Sure. Of course.

JAQ: I wanted to kill myself.

PRESIDENT: Did you. Do you—is that something you still . . .

JAQ: I've worked very hard to address the underlying issues.

PRESIDENT: Well that's great to hear. And our, hopefully our counseling services have been responsive to you, if that's where you—

JAQ: I didn't seek treatment there because I didn't feel they were knowledgeable about—

ELLEN: This is an issue the committee has—

PROVOST: Certainly our counseling services need to be educated about all—

PRESIDENT: That's an important—I mean Ellen, and Jaq, hearing you say that—ever read Camus?

(Pause.)

JAQ: I have not.

PRESIDENT: Anyone?

GABE: I have.

PRESIDENT: What about you, Jay?

JAY: I've read some . . .

PRESIDENT: Well let me ask you two—since Ellen brought it up— do you ever think about suicide?

JAY: I've—definitely been depressed at times . . .

GABE: In high school I did . . .

PRESIDENT: Now Ellen, I don't want to take anything away from what you—I bring up Camus because—we're a university, we have two goals as I see it: to educate you and to take care of you en route your becoming an adult—and I think one of the ways we do that is by caring for your emotional needs— including the need to experience the world free from discrim- ination and prejudice—but I can answer the question too and say—No, I don't think about suicide now—but I did when I was younger—and I think part of what's interesting to me about what we have to do—it's not that I object to your, to the conclusions you draw, Ellen—I'm sure despair fastens to whatever is unique about a person's life experience—but sui- cide is a very common—when people are young and trying to understand themselves and the world—it's a very existential thing—it's part of coming to terms with being thrown into the world against your will, the pain of—correct me if I'm wrong but unless I'm misremembering, Camus wrote about this—am I—

GABE: —that suicide is the only real philosophical question.

PRESIDENT: Yes. Now that's—in Camus's view, a necessary step to—

ELLEN: I understand your point, but I am reading papers from my students and it's not an existential dilemma causing them to consider suicide. It's the structural oppression they are facing at every level of university life—in dorms, in classrooms, in public spaces—

PRESIDENT: And that's why I said I'm committed—I wasn't trying to be flippant—I'm just saying, we're at a university—I remember staying up all night my freshman year reading Shakespeare and realizing—life is tragic! We have to prepare our kids for that fact!

ELLEN: Everyone knows life is tragic—

PRESIDENT: Do our students know? "Kids today"—I hate that phrase—but *do* they?

PROVOST: I do think that we can do both—encourage students to think in the deepest ways about the problems of living—while ensuring they feel safe enough to do that.

ELLEN: Those goals are actually interdependent. If a student doesn't feel safe he or she *can't*—

PRESIDENT: This might sound like a strange question—but have the three of you met before today?

(Pause.)

There's your answer.

ELLEN: Oppressed groups frequently internalize their oppression—

PRESIDENT: Come on, don't intellectualize—

ELLEN: I'm not—

PRESIDENT: Why aren't the three of you friends? Or at least why don't you know each other?

(Pause.)

JAQ: There aren't really opportunities . . .

PRESIDENT: What about—isn't there a dance coming up? Queer Students—right? You guys going?

GABE: Well—I have to, since I'm the—

PRESIDENT: Okay—Jaq?

JAQ: It's not my thing.

PRESIDENT: Why not?

JAQ: It's a very—no offense—*homogeneous* group—

GABE: No, I—we've tried to make it more inclusive—

JAQ: It's not your fault—

PRESIDENT: Jay?

JAY: The one time I went to a club, a group of guys asked me if my penis worked—so—

JAQ: That sounds like things people say to me. Horrible.

PRESIDENT: All right, so—but this should be a friendly—right—or even if it isn't fully—you guys know each other now—and if you bring your friends—my point is, we're going to be adopting a lot of the Social Justice Committee recommendations—

ELLEN: Which ones?

PRESIDENT: Come on, you know I can't tell you now—but that's all—top-down stuff—

ELLEN: You know, I do enjoy these entertaining, freewheeling conversations—

PRESIDENT: But let me finish, Ellen—a lot of this stuff has to be grassroots. Change happens both ways—I could make a joke there—won't—but if a big part of the problem is you guys not talking to one another—then start!

ELLEN: But they don't know each other. They don't feel safe or included—even where they should. That's why I'm reading essays about students wanting to kill themselves—

PRESIDENT: If they want to kill themselves, why aren't they talking about that with—

JAQ: Oh wow. I just got sent this article that came out in the *Daily*—it says Kevin Gillman was gay.

(Pause. Everyone takes out smartphones.)

PRESIDENT: "The Mystery of a Suicide" . . . huh.

ELLEN: There's an editorial, too: "If true, this brings up questions about the climate at the university and what more can be done to encourage closeted students to seek—"

PRESIDENT: And that's an important—that's something we certainly have to address, I agree—now—I don't know how people are feeling right now—it's clear we're all very engrossed in reading . . . Two options as I see it—this is obviously a big story, we're all feeling the impact of it . . . if people want to go do their own thing now—I'd understand that . . .

ELLEN: I think this changes things. It puts a face to something that hasn't had a face here—

PRESIDENT: If people want time to process before talking further—what we can do is reconvene—

PROVOST: We can have the President's office schedule a follow-up meeting—

PRESIDENT: Because I think it's important that we keep meeting—

ELLEN: A lot of students are going to want to talk about this article—

PRESIDENT: Maybe we can even create a space for that today—

PROVOST: Certainly—

PRESIDENT: Any other thoughts from anyone?

(Pause.)

GABE: Well I hope the dance party—can serve as a—if we get a good turnout—and it's a diverse group of students—that that can be a first step in building a better community—

PRESIDENT: Absolutely. Jay, Jaq—is that something that—would you guys consider going?

JAQ: I—to be honest, probably not.

PRESIDENT: Okay. Jay?

JAY: I'll—give it a shot—

GABE: Thanks.

PRESIDENT: Great. All right, everybody—so—we'll be in touch and meet up again very soon.

ELLEN: Thank you—this is a real opportunity.

PRESIDENT: I agree.

(All but President and Provost exit.)

This article seems pretty thin, right?

PROVOST: On facts. But it might make a real impact. He was a very popular figure on campus.

PRESIDENT: I don't see how you can say someone killed themselves just because they're gay. This whole generation being educated into this simplistic way of thinking . . .

PROVOST: How should we respond?

PRESIDENT: Let's have some kind of forum . . . Where everyone can say what a horrible place this is.

2.5

DREW: Hey, thanks for coming—

GABE: Of course—what's going on?

DREW: I know you're busy getting stuff ready for the—

GABE: No—

DREW: Do you want anything to drink?

GABE: Sure—whatever—

DREW: So the lunch was good?

GABE: Yeah, I mean—the more I think about it—I don't know—
but what's going on with you?

DREW: I know, sorry for being so dramatic—

GABE: It's okay—you seemed really down in your texts, what's—

DREW: We'll talk about it. But the more you think about the
lunch . . . ?

GABE: Just—listening to other people talk—there's, like, this victim thing that really bugs me . . .

DREW: What do you mean?

GABE: I just—this idea that the university's to blame for all this
stuff, that it's so homophobic—

DREW: You mean—are you talking about the article?

GABE: No, no—just the way they spoke—it was really arrogant and whiny, like—

DREW: I don't understand—

GABE: A couple of them were just very dramatic. Like our school is this horrible, oppressive—

DREW: But—it is for some people—

GABE: No, I know—

DREW: You're a very strong person. You came out in high school. Not everyone is like you—

GABE: Yeah, but . . . like, the person there who probably has it the toughest—this guy who's in a wheelchair—he didn't come off like a victim at all. Meanwhile this tenured professor is—

DREW: But wait, just—are you saying you disagree with the editorial I wrote?

GABE: No—like I texted you, I thought both the article and the editorial were really good—

DREW: So what are you saying then?

GABE: I'm—I'm not explaining myself well—

DREW: Yeah—maybe you should stop trying.

(Pause.)

GABE: Sorry—

DREW: No, I'm just—in a bad mood—

GABE: What's going on?

DREW: I don't know. I think I'm depressed. I guess I just expected . . . I don't know. I don't really want to talk about it.

GABE: But . . . you asked me to come over—to talk about it, didn't you?

DREW: I don't know.

(Pause.)

GABE: I mean we don't have to but . . .

DREW: Will you rub my feet?

GABE: Sure.

DREW: Wanna watch something?

GABE: TV?

DREW: Yeah.

GABE: I mean—we hadn't planned on hanging out tonight so—I do have a lot of work to do—I'm not sure how long I can—

DREW: Well you came over—how long *can* you stay?

GABE: I mean—I just meant I don't know if it's the best use of time to watch—

DREW: You really want me to talk?

GABE: Yeah—you said you're depressed.

DREW: Well you don't like whiners or victims so . . .

(Pause.)

GABE: That's not what I meant.

DREW: What did you mean?

GABE: No, you're not—like them, you're not, like, *haughty*. It was mostly the way they spoke . . .

(Pause.)

DREW: I think I just expected more response to the article.

GABE: Really? But it just came out—

DREW: Nothing will change. Nothing ever changes.

GABE: They already had that open forum tonight—

DREW: I don't just mean here—in general. Gay marriage could become legal everywhere, it will still be bad to be gay. It will always be this horrible thing you have to go through—

GABE: Look how much things have changed in just ten years, though—

DREW: Gay kids are still getting bullied all over the place. No one cares—

GABE: Is it that—did you think something specific would happen once the article came out?

DREW: Like what?

GABE: I don't know—

DREW: You're really good at that, you know.

GABE: What? Foot massage?

DREW: Yeah. How do you know how to do it so well?

GABE: Dunno—instinct I guess.

DREW: You never learned how to do it?

GABE: No.

DREW: It's so nice.

GABE: Thanks.

DREW: Never got me hard before . . .

(Pause.)

GABE: Oh yeah?

(Drew reaches for Gabe.)

Hey—we're in the middle of—

DREW: I wanna have sex—

GABE: Yeah, but—

DREW: I don't want to talk anymore about it—

GABE: But we should—

(Drew climbs on top of Gabe.)

Drew!

DREW: What? God!

GABE: I want to finish the—

DREW: You really want to talk? Because other guys haven't wanted to. Even when they said they did.

(Pause.)

GABE: Well I do.

(Pause.)

DREW: I sent the article and the editorial to my mom and dad. You know, like—this is something I brought into the world, this is a really big deal—

GABE: Yeah—

DREW: My dad wrote, "Will read this later." Which means he'll never read it.

GABE: Really?

DREW: He's just selfish. I mean he cheated on my mother all growing up—

GABE: He did?

DREW: And his new wife hates me so he just goes through the motions, you know?

GABE: I'm sorry.

DREW: My *mom* . . . read it. And called me . . .

GABE: What did she say?

DREW: Nothing. She didn't mention it.

GABE: At all?

DREW: She texted me, "Read the article, will call you later." When she *called*, all she talked about is this guy she's dating and how she can't tell if he's really serious or not.

GABE: Did you ask her about it?

DREW: No—by that point I just wanted to get off the phone.

GABE: That really sucks.

DREW: And I guess I thought—some newspapers or TV stations would call, pick the story up . . .

GABE: They might still—it's only been out eight hours—

DREW: But remember how big a story his suicide was last year? It was huge!

GABE: Give it time . . .

(Pause.)

DREW: What did I do to deserve you?

GABE: What do you mean? You were you.

DREW: That's it?

GABE: That's it.

DREW: Probably didn't hurt that I'm sexy.

GABE: Ha. That's part of you.

DREW: How big a part?

GABE: I don't know . . .

DREW: There'll be hot guys at the dance party . . .

GABE: Well—I mean—

DREW: What about when you see them?

GABE: I asked you to come!

DREW: But you knew I wasn't going to—

GABE: I'd never cheat on you.

DREW: Every gay guy cheats.

GABE: Whoa—you really believe that?

DREW: Yeah. Gay culture is practically built around it.

GABE: Does that mean—do you cheat?

DREW: I've never done it, but . . . I have really bad abandonment issues. If I felt like I was going to be—I don't know. I might. I'm sorry, I'm fucking everything up—

GABE: No—listen. You don't need to be scared of me. Okay?

(Pause. Drew climbs on top of Gabe.)

DREW: I want you so fucking much—

3.1

TIM: Okay, I'm officially pissed off.

JENNY: Forty-five minutes late, you're allowed.

TIM: This guy is a nightmare. Why is he so into him?

JENNY: Should we just leave?

TIM: He said he's still coming . . .

JENNY: He won't have much time before the dance party.

TIM: He'll have time for a drink or two. —So I guess we're not going?

JENNY: I have stuff to do . . .

TIM: I could always go for a little while I guess. Just to be supportive . . .

(Pause.)

JENNY: Are you okay?

TIM: Yeah, why?

JENNY: You seem like you've been in a bad mood recently.

TIM: I'm all right.

JENNY: Nothing's going on?

TIM: No . . .

(Pause. Gabe enters.)

GABE: Hey, sorry—

TIM: Hey!

JENNY: What's going on?

GABE: Who knows. I was getting ready to go meet him when he texted me and said he felt *sick* and didn't think he should go out. I asked him if he needed anything or wanted me to come over—he said *no*. So I said okay, I'd call him later. Then I get this text saying *Wow.*

TIM: Just wow?

GABE: Just wow. So I text him a question mark. He texts back *Thanks for all your support.*

TIM: He told you he didn't need anything.

GABE: I know! So then we got into this whole thing—he has abandonment issues and I guess being sick—he just felt sort of abandoned by me—

TIM: But you offered to go over—

GABE: That's what I told him!

JENNY: He was probably just embarrassed to ask you and was hoping you'd just do it.

TIM: If I were him I'd be more embarrassed to throw a fit after telling someone—

JENNY: Abandonment is a big thing though—

TIM: So how did it resolve?

GABE: I ended up going over there and—I think I calmed him down.

TIM: How did you do that? Unless it's X-rated.

GABE: Same thing I did last night, just rubbed his feet for a little while.

TIM: PG-13.

GABE: He *seemed* okay when I left—anyway . . .

TIM: Want a drink? Usual?

GABE: *Yes.*

(Tim goes.)

JENNY: Well you're here now!

GABE: I really wanted him to meet you guys . . . —I think he's threatened by Tim.

JENNY: Why?

GABE: He has this crazy idea that Tim is—attracted to me.

JENNY: Based on what?

GABE: No idea! I don't think he has many straight friends, I don't think he understands . . .

    What?

JENNY: Before he gets back—I have to ask you something. I'm kind of going crazy.

GABE: What?

JENNY: I think Tim is cheating on me.

    You wouldn't know something like that and not tell me, would you?

GABE: No—of course not. But he'd never . . .

JENNY: You really don't think he would?

GABE: No, I—why do you think that?

JENNY: It's like he's annoyed whenever we're together. He's going running all the time . . .

(Pause.)

GABE: It's probably just senior year—being stressed about the future—

JENNY: Just promise me—if you know something—you'll tell me.

GABE: No, yeah—

JENNY: He's coming—

(Tim enters.)

TIM: So I have something to ask. That article—what's up with that?

(Pause.)

GABE: The one about Kevin Gillman?

TIM: It was kind of crazy I thought! I mean I didn't know the guy well but—and not that he ever would have flirted with me—

GABE: That's right, he was on the Student Assembly—

TIM: That dude definitely didn't seem gay.

JENNY: You think you can tell just by looking?

GABE: Yeah, thanks—

TIM: No, I'm—it just seemed like wish fulfillment to me. Like it really *wanted* him to be gay. Hot guy, super popular, hot girl-friend—it was like that gay porn site you told me about—

GABE: Tim!

TIM: What? Everybody's looked at porn.

JENNY: But—you don't just *say* it—

TIM: Whatever—you told me it claims the guys are straight—you said it was super popular—

GABE: Yeah but—there *are* closeted guys—the article is not making up that phenomenon.

TIM: Okay, fine, guess you never know.

I don't look at porn. Promise.

JENNY: All right, can we—

TIM: I mean sometimes when your girlfriend goes to Europe for all of August—*maybe*—

JENNY: Tim—

GABE: So are you guys coming to the dance party?

TIM: Are we coming to the dance party . . .

JENNY: I—what are we . . .

GABE: Ugh! I just talked to him! —One second, sorry—

(Gabe goes.)

JENNY: Why would you say that? You embarrassed him.

TIM: He's the one who told me about it—

JENNY: Not in front of me. And you embarrassed me, too!

TIM: I was just—making a joke.

JENNY: It's disrespectful.

TIM: Okay. Sorry.

So you're not going to the . . .

JENNY: No.

Are you?

(Pause.)

TIM: No . . .

JENNY: You wanna come over?

TIM: After this I'm just gonna call it a night I think. I'm tired.

(Gabe returns.)

GABE: He wants me to check in a few times over the course of the night.

TIM: That's nice. Stands you up and now wants to ruin your party!

JENNY: He's probably just nervous about you being at a gay club without him.

GABE: I'm starting to think he should be.

TIM: Whoa!

GABE: Whatever—so how drunk should I get before going to the club?

TIM: *Very.*

3.2

TEDDY (*On his computer as before*): So far it's three that I go to the party, nineteen that I cam . . .

I gotta decide soon, get your votes in! Twenty . . .

I still haven't seen him. No, we texted. I asked him for the room again between nine and eleven and he said okay. At nine I checked his camera and it was *on again*. So I looked at his Twitter and he was like, *It's happening again, if you wanna watch DM me!*

Got another screenshot, sent it to my RA. He's totally busted. I just don't know how long it takes to—

You're voting on—thank you for explaining—

The guy was awesome. Better than last time. Definitely be seeing him again. No, I just unplugged his computer and made sure there were no other hidden cams . . .

The votes are piling up . . . you guys really want to watch me jerk off . . .

(*Pause.*)

No, nothing—just distracted . . .

(Pause.)

I'm gonna go to the party. Sorry. —There are four hundred other cams you can look at!

I'll be back. You'll see me jerk it again. Later, studs—

(Teddy shuts down the computer.)

3.3

JAY *(Approaches Gabe)*: Hey—

GABE: Hi! You came!

JAY: I'm a man of my word!

GABE: That's great! Decent turnout . . .

JAY: Yeah, looks like it!

GABE: Have you been out there yet?

JAY: Not yet . . .

GABE: You'll dance, though, right?

JAY: Let's see how drunk I get . . .

GABE: Aw, you don't need to be drunk to dance! We'll get you out there.

JAY: Well look who's talking!

GABE: Right—the texting never ends—so that was a crazy meeting yesterday!

JAY: I know! Is he out of his mind or what?

GABE: Actually—I kind of like the guy!

JAY: Ha! Really?

GABE: He speaks his mind!

JAY: But he's a total jackass!

(Teddy enters at the far corner.)

GABE: No, I hear you.

JAY: You think we'll actually have a follow-up?

GABE: Oh, there's—sorry, I just saw someone I need to—

JAY: Okay—

GABE: Don't go anywhere—or, if you do—I'll find you—*on* the dance floor hopefully!

JAY: Well then I definitely need to go get another drink . . .

GABE: Ha!

(Gabe goes to Teddy. Jay exits.)

Hey!

TEDDY: Hi—

GABE: You came!

TEDDY: Yup. —Taking a break from dancing?

GABE: Oh—just texting with my boyfriend—

TEDDY: He's not here?

GABE: No, he—he's the editor of the *Daily*, you know—

TEDDY: Oh—

GABE: And there was this big story yesterday—

TEDDY: Yeah I saw it.

GABE: So—he's busy working . . .

TEDDY: Did you know—

GABE: Sorry?

TEDDY: No, I saw—on this site—guys, like, hook up—in the library bathroom—

GABE: Oh—yeah. I'm sorry I haven't messaged you yet—

TEDDY: It's okay—that guy came over again tonight.

GABE: What?

TEDDY: I had a date with this—

GABE: Right, right—sorry, I'm a little—

TEDDY: My roommate tried to use his webcam, like, to watch us.

GABE: Wait—what?

TEDDY: Second time. Pointed his webcam at my side of the room so he could view it remotely—

GABE: Are you *serious*?

TEDDY: He, like, broadcast it—he told people about it on Facebook, Twitter—

GABE: Jesus—did you go to your RA?

TEDDY: Yeah, and two people above him. I have screencaps—

GABE: That's insane. Are you—okay?

TEDDY: He couldn't see much the first time, the second time I figured it out before anything—

GABE: But—do you feel safe there? What will you do while the university—

TEDDY: I can handle myself—I don't think he'll do it again. What did you text your boyfriend?

GABE: What did I—uh—just that I miss him . . .

TEDDY: You told him you miss him?

GABE: Yeah. Which is kind of a lie honestly!

TEDDY: Ha . . . do you . . .

GABE: Sorry, I couldn't . . .

TEDDY: No, it's hard to—I still have these canker sores—I'm not talking clearly—

(Jay enters with drink.)

GABE: Well—I'm gonna get back to my friend—but I'll see you on the dance floor!

(Gabe goes over to Jay.)

Got your drink!

JAY: I did!

GABE: Drink it fast, I want to dance!

JAY: Don't mind me . . .

GABE: Stop, we're getting you out there!

(Teddy exits.)

Oh you know what—I just want to ask that guy his last name—

(Gabe turns.)

Shit, he—Ted, Teddy . . . I'm supposed to add him on Facebook—

CHRISTOPHER SHINN

JAY: I don't know him—

GABE: I keep forgetting to do it and then when I remember I can't remember his last name—

(Nicky approaches.)

NICKY: Hi!

GABE: Hi—do I know you?

NICKY: Not really—I'm Nicky—I write for the *Daily*, I wrote the piece on Kevin Gillman—

GABE: Oh—so you know—

NICKY: Drew—very well!

GABE: This is my friend Jay—we were both in the President's office actually when the article—

NICKY: Drew told me that—anyway—I saw you, I just wanted to introduce myself—I'm just here to have a good time, not doing anything for the *Daily*—

GABE: That's good—

NICKY: Drew didn't send me to spy on you, I swear—

GABE: Ha! Well I think Jay and I are gonna hit the dance floor—yeah?

JAY: What the hell.

GABE: Nice meeting you!

(They turn to go. Nicky grabs Gabe. Jay continues off.)

NICKY: I just wanted to say—I kind of feel like I know you, even though we've never—

GABE: Oh yeah?

NICKY: Just—Drew can be really demanding, I'm sure you have your own experience of that—

GABE: Uh-huh—

NICKY: Not in a *bad* way—he gets results!

GABE: Right—

NICKY: I mean—I'm just imagining what it's like to date him, obviously I don't *know*—

GABE: Well—I won't totally disabuse you of your impression—

NICKY: That's good—I'd much rather be *abused* than *disabused*—

GABE: Ah!

TEDDY FERRARA

65

NICKY: Sorry—

GABE: Hey, no—flirt all you want—not like my boyfriend's around!

NICKY: Please, he's *always* around!

GABE: God, don't say that—does he text you a lot, too?

NICKY: It's *so* controlling, isn't it?

GABE: Well—I'm gonna let the beat control me. Nice meeting you!

> *(Gabe goes off.*
> *Teddy enters. He goes toward Nicky.)*

TEDDY: Hey.

> *(Nicky goes off.*
> *Teddy exits.)*

3.4

TIM (*Grabs Gabe*): YO!

GABE: —WHOA!

TIM: I'M DANCING, BABY!

GABE: I CAN'T BELIEVE YOU'RE HERE! AND DANCING—

TIM: JENNY'S COMING, TOO, I TEXTED HER—

GABE: SHE IS?

TIM: I WAS SO CLOSE TO HOOKING UP WITH THAT GIRL, DUDE—I DON'T KNOW WHAT'S HAPPENING TO ME—

GABE: SERIOUSLY?

TIM: SHE KEEPS MESSAGING ME—SHE'S SO FUCKING HOT!

GABE: DON'T CHEAT ON JENNY!

TIM: I'M NOT—THAT'S WHY I CAME HERE, SO I WOULDN'T—

GABE: BUT I DON'T UNDERSTAND WHY YOU—

TIM: EVER SINCE SHE GOT BACK FROM EUROPE IT'S BEEN WEIRD—

GABE: HOW?

TIM: DUNNO! IT'S HARD TO EXPLAIN—

(*Jay nears, dancing in his wheelchair.*)

GABE: HAVE YOU GUYS TALKED ABOUT IT?

TIM: NO—SO YOUR MAN NEVER SHOWED UP?

GABE: NO! HE KEEPS TEXTING ME—

TIM: TURN OFF YOUR PHONE! IF HE WANTS YOU HE CAN COME AND GET YOU!

YOU'RE A GOOD DANCER!

GABE: THANKS! SO ARE YOU!

TIM: HEY, DID WE EVER MAKE OUT?

GABE: WHAT—HOW DRUNK ARE YOU?!

TIM: I WAS REMEMBERING FRESHMAN YEAR—DIDN'T WE GET DARED?

GABE: I THINK YOU'VE LOST YOUR MIND!

TIM: I REMEMBER US PLAYING TRUTH OR DARE—I'M SO FUCKING WASTED!

GABE: GEE, REALLY?

TIM: I CAN'T BELIEVE HOW CLOSE I WAS TO HOOKING UP WITH THAT GIRL, DUDE—

(Jenny enters.)

JENNY: HEY!

TIM: YOU GOT HERE FAST!

GABE: HEY JENNY!

JENNY: THERE'S A LOT OF PEOPLE HERE! YOU MUST BE HAPPY!

GABE: IT'S PRETTY AWESOME!

(Tim and Jenny start dancing. Gabe sees Jay.)

WE'RE GETTING YOU LAID TONIGHT!

JAY: WHAT?

GABE: *WE'RE GETTING YOU LAID!*

JAY: YOU'RE CRAZY!

GABE: WE GOT YOU DANCING, DIDN'T WE?

JAY: YEAH BUT I CAN DANCE ALONE!

GABE: WE'RE GONNA MAKE IT HAPPEN! —CHRIST! MY BOY-FRIEND WON'T STOP TEXTING ME!

JAY: REALLY?

GABE: FUCK IT—I'M TURNING OFF MY PHONE! SO ARE YOU FUCKED UP?

JAY: PRETTY FUCKED UP—

GABE: I AM FUCKED *UP!*

3.5

TEDDY (*Holding phone, recording*): At the library . . . looking down . . .
from the balcony . . .

    Fifteen minutes to closing . . . pretty quiet . . .

    Guys get blowjobs in that bathroom . . . under the stall
dividers . . .

    (*Looks at phone; erases, records again*) Library . . . ninth
floor . . . That's me, hello . . .

    (*Erases, records again*) At the library . . .

    (*Erases, records again*) Hello. I'm Mr. Canker Sore!

    (*Erases, records again*) Library . . .

(*He erases. Types something into his phone.*
    He drops the phone off the balcony, watches it.)

Yup.

(*He jumps.*)

3.6

JENNY: Whose idea was it to walk?

TIM: Just don't fall on your face on the concrete—cuz then I'd have to dump you.

JENNY: Fuck you!

TIM: Hey, it was Gabe's idea to walk when none of us are capable of it—er—sorry, I—

JAY: It's okay—

TIM: I didn't mean to—

JAY: It's totally fine—

GABE: Wouldn't you rather barf in the bushes than all over your friends in the back of a cab?

JENNY: The last time I was in a cab the BO alone made me want to hurl. It wasn't even summer!

GABE: Why don't some people bathe?

TIM: And by some people you mean Indians—

JAY: Okay, *that* is offensive—

TIM: It's true!

GABE: Not all Indians—

TIM: Just Indian cab drivers—whoa—I actually I think need to go throw up—

JENNY: I'll go with you—
TIM: That's okay—I'll text you if I start choking to death—
JENNY: Don't make jokes!

(Tim goes off. Gabe turns on phone.)

GABE: So we didn't get you laid, Jay!
JAY: No . . . no one wants to have sex with people in wheelchairs.

(Sounds of vomiting from off.)

JENNY: I'm gonna go make sure he's—

(Jenny goes off. Gabe looks at his phone.)

JAY: I had a great time, though. I had so much fun dancing . . .
    Everything okay?
GABE: I . . .

(Jenny and Tim return.)

TIM: Highly recommend those bushes—very accommodating.
JENNY: You love a nice bush—
GABE: Drew just dumped me.

(Pause.)

TIM: What?
GABE: Sent me a text like an hour ago: "I don't think we should see
    each other anymore."
JENNY: That's it? Out of nowhere?
GABE: "Sorry." That's it.
    Why would he . . . What—
TIM: Fuck that guy, dude—
GABE: I . . .

(Pause.)

JENNY: Look—police up there . . .

3.7

Nicky takes pictures with his phone. Police cross.

NICKY: Excuse me—I'm with the *Daily*—
POLICE 1: You want to make sure—people are gonna—
POLICE 2: Yeah—

(Police 1 goes off.)

NICKY: Is there anything you can—
POLICE 2: There's been an incident but that's all I can say.
NICKY: Why is there an ambulance?
POLICE 2: That's all I can say.

(Gabe, Jay, Tim and Jenny enter. Nicky goes to them.)

GABE: Do you know what happened?
NICKY: They won't say anything—I was walking back from the—

(Police 2 is called on his walkie-talkie, exits.)

GABE: That's a lot of—could it be a shooting—
NICKY: It doesn't seem like it's still going on—the police seem pretty calm, I haven't gotten any emergency text messages from the university, have you guys?
TIM: No . . . It's probably nothing—
NICKY: I'm gonna try to find out more—

(Nicky goes off.)

JAY: You think someone jumped?

(Pause.)

GABE: Jesus—
JENNY: Like a copycat thing—
TIM: They call ambulances just to be safe—probably someone fell, or passed out—
NICKY *(Entering quickly)*: My friend just texted me—a freshman posted on his Facebook that he was jumping off the ninth floor of the library.
GABE: What?
NICKY: Literally, like, ten or fifteen minutes ago—he sent me the screenshot—
GABE: Does it say who it was?
NICKY: Ted something—
GABE: Ted?
NICKY *(Looks on phone)*: Let me—
GABE: Ted Ferrara?
NICKY: Yeah.

4.1

PRESIDENT: Well. We're not all here. But should we get started?

PROVOST: Has anyone heard from Gabe?

(Pause.)

PRESIDENT: I mean I'm tempted to—usually I'd say let's just start—
but in light of—I mean, is anyone—I don't know if anyone here
really knows him at all—but is anyone concerned? . . .

JAY: I've—been in touch with him.

PRESIDENT: Did you expect him to be here today?

JAY: I did . . .

PRESIDENT: Twenty minutes late—does that concern you?

JAY: I can't imagine anything—he's been a little depressed but—

ELLEN: Well can we call him?

PROVOST: The office has been trying to contact him—

JAY: I texted him right before the meeting . . .

PRESIDENT: Okay. Well look—it's probably nothing—I just wanted
to be—we can start—

ELLEN: But wait—I think this is a perfect example of not talking about something we should be able to talk about. You just said he's been depressed . . .

JAY: We were—supposed to go to the vigil together last night, but at the last minute he just said he didn't feel like going, he didn't feel like being public . . .

ELLEN: You know, we overlook these signs of depression and then—things like Teddy Ferrara—

PRESIDENT: Well what do you want us to do, Ellen?

ELLEN: At the least, not be afraid to talk about it. All these fears about privacy, overstepping—why can't we talk about someone's pain? Why can't we care about each other?

PRESIDENT: We are talking about it.

ELLEN: No, you wanted to start the meeting and change the subject—

JAQ: I think we do avoid talking about difficult things.

ELLEN: I mean, not going to the vigil—are there any other signs that he's depressed, Jay?

JAY: Well I just . . . I know his boyfriend—broke up with him and . . . he had filed to run for Student Assembly President but wasn't sure if—he had to decide Friday whether to withdraw . . . he just seemed like—

ELLEN: So—it sounds like he was separating himself from student life because of—

JAY: He wasn't really in touch over the weekend except to say he wasn't going to the vigil—

ELLEN: These are a lot of signs. This is someone we as a community should be concerned about—

(Gabe enters.)

GABE: Sorry I'm late—

PRESIDENT: Hi Gabe. So we're all here. Have a seat.

So. Obviously the—I can't believe it isn't even a week ago that we met. There was a sense of immediacy then—now the immediacy has an immediacy. I'd like to—

ELLEN: Can we talk about the rumors about this roommate issue Teddy had?

PROVOST: It's both a criminal investigation as well as something the Office of Student Conduct is—

ELLEN: I know you can't "say" anything—but come on. This is an off-the-record—

PRESIDENT: You know I love opening my big mouth. But we really can't—

PROVOST: Unfortunately we can't—

ELLEN: Because you're scared of lawsuits.

PROVOST: The protocol is—

ELLEN: You've invited us to speak frankly—

PRESIDENT: There are some things we just can't comment on. Come on, you know that—

ELLEN: Well let's talk about what you *can* say. Not about the—but to address publicly what is now undeniable, which is that the climate for queer students at this university is *deadly*.

(Pause.)

PRESIDENT: I have some ideas. But tell me what you'd like me to say.

ELLEN: You're not going to say what I want you to say.

PRESIDENT: But I'd like to know what you—and frankly, Ellen, you don't know that.

JAQ: I know what I'd like you to say.

PRESIDENT: Great, what is that?

JAQ: People are expecting you to say how sad this, what a tragedy, we all have to come together—

PRESIDENT: Honestly, I don't want to say that stuff, any more than you want me to—

JAQ: Well—I think you should challenge your audience. Say, "The hate that killed Teddy Ferrara is in your heart. Every one of you. Maybe there's not that much of it, maybe you've worked hard to eliminate discrimination in yourself, but it's still there a little bit. And that's the part of yourself you need to be thinking about right now. Not the ninety-nine percent that wants queer students to live. The one percent that wants them to die."

(Pause.)

PRESIDENT: You really think most people at this university want queer students to *die*?

JAQ: A part of them—yes. Yes I do.

PRESIDENT: Jay—what would you like to hear me say?

JAY: I think anytime there's an expectation that an authority is going to speak in clichés or platitudes—there's a real opportunity to say something original and shake things up—

JAQ: Exactly—

JAY: To the extent that there is a culture of homophobia here . . . It is important to address that.

PRESIDENT: Gabe?

GABE: I don't think you should say anything until we have all the facts.

(Pause.)

ELLEN: A gay student who was being bullied by his roommate and dorm mates is dead.

GABE: Right—but lots of gay students are bullied and don't kill themselves.

ELLEN: What's your point?

GABE: There might be other reasons he killed himself as well. Nobody knows—

ELLEN: There might be a thousand reasons. But bullying is obviously a primary—

PRESIDENT: All right—that's Gabe's point of view—

ELLEN: Do you find that a compelling point of view?

PRESIDENT: Ellen—I'm committed to addressing this problem. I was before Teddy Ferrara died—

ELLEN: So we're airing out all these points of view—what are you going to say?

PRESIDENT: Well look—we need to strategize the best way to go about laying the groundwork for—

ELLEN: This is such bullshit. If the institution sends the signal that this is not really a pressing—

JAQ: It has to be a priority—

PRESIDENT: It is! But if bullying is as big a problem as you're saying—we can't wave a magic wand—

ELLEN: So what's the point of this meeting? To pacify us? To buy time?

PROVOST: In addition to speeding up implementing Social Justice Committee recommendations—there is an opportunity to speak forthrightly—if we can find the best way to do that—

ELLEN: I think you should immediately announce an effort to address social justice that will *require* participation from all faculty, students and administrators—details to follow.

JAQ: One thing you could do right away is fund a safe space for anyone, if they're being bullied, for them to go to and talk to someone who has institutional authority—

ELLEN: That seems uncontroversial to me—I don't think you need to "lay the groundwork"—

PRESIDENT: We—listen. We're going to do things. But truly *changing* the culture is not an overnight—

ELLEN: No one said it's overnight! But that doesn't mean it needs to take ten years—

PRESIDENT: I agree—all I was—look, I think you've both made important suggestions. Gabe?

GABE: I think the most important message the university can send right now is that it doesn't accept students committing suicide in its buildings.

PRESIDENT: What do you mean?

GABE: Put up barriers on the upper balconies of the library so people can't jump off them.

JAQ: But—if you want to kill yourself you'll just do it some other way—

GABE: But it sends a message: two students have done this and we don't accept it.

JAQ: That doesn't make any sense.

GABE: You don't know that he would have killed himself some other way—maybe not.

JAQ: But that doesn't have anything to do with the underlying problem of discrimination.

GABE: No, it has to do with trying to prevent more suicides by saying, "You may not do this."

JAQ: But if you don't address why students are—

GABE: We don't know why.

(*Pause.*)

PRESIDENT: This is a little off topic, but did you—the Police Chief just told me that—men have sex in the library bathrooms— and on that floor, the ninth floor, where Teddy jumped from.

GABE: That's true. It's a well-known cruising spot.

PRESIDENT: This strikes me as something that we should stop—it sends a strange message, doesn't it, to gay students—that gay people need to do this distasteful thing in secret, illicitly—

ELLEN: There are very complex reasons that men have anonymous sex. There's a long history—

PRESIDENT: Sure—twenty, thirty years ago, I get it. But now? In this day and age?

ELLEN: If criminalizing gay activity is what you're taking away from—

PRESIDENT: First of all, it's already illegal—you can't have sex in a public—

ELLEN: Consensual sex in public restrooms did not cause Teddy Ferrara to—

PRESIDENT: What if one reason he killed himself is, he thought— that's my future. That's being gay.

GABE: I think that's a really good point.

ELLEN: That, to me, is absurd.

PRESIDENT: I was shocked to hear about it. I mean it's disgusting—

ELLEN: I cannot believe this is what we're talking about—

PRESIDENT: It's not what I'm—look, today is a busy—we need to wrap things up—

ELLEN: This weekend is Homecoming. This is the one time the entire university comes together as a community. If you can use this opportunity to speak to everyone—

JAQ: I think it should be during the game. At halftime, there should be a ceremony—

PRESIDENT: Maybe at the *Beach Crew* show, too! Joking—that was a joke—

ELLEN: I know you appreciate forthrightness, which is why I've been forthright.

PRESIDENT: I do. We are going to respond to this aggressively. You have my word.

ELLEN: Well, we'll see. But thank you.

PRESIDENT: All right. Thank you, guys, for coming.

JAQ: Any news on running for Senate?

PRESIDENT: You'll be the first to know, Jaq.

PROVOST: Thank you, everyone.

PRESIDENT: Gabe, hang back a second, there's something I wanted to ask you . . .

(All exit save Gabe and President.)

GABE: Sorry I was late—this reporter got my number and I couldn't get off the phone—

PRESIDENT: Ahh, yes. Reporters.

GABE: You probably have a lot of experience—

PRESIDENT: That I do. If you can master the skill of speaking to them while you're young—maybe you can actually be President one day instead of just a university President!

GABE: Ha—it must not be easy having to watch what you say.

PRESIDENT: It's the price you pay for being someone people will listen to. So listen—we were chatting earlier, and Jay mentioned you'd been thinking about withdrawing from running for Student Assembly President.

GABE: Oh—I did think about it. But I decided to stay in the race.

PRESIDENT: Oh, great! We need students like you getting involved—people with a point of view.

GABE: There's a rumor you're going to be at the candidates' forum tomorrow.

PRESIDENT: I will be! I think it's a good way of showing that we take the Student Assembly seriously. And after what happened Thursday night—it's good that I be visible.

GABE: I agree. Well—I'll see you there!

PRESIDENT: Excellent.

(Gabe goes. Provost returns.)

PROVOST: Any thoughts?

PRESIDENT: I like that kid.

PROVOST: There's a surprise.

PRESIDENT: Hey, he's saying things that are true! You can tell Ellen thinks this is her moment—we really need charges to be filed on the roommate. It's gonna be tense till then.

CHRISTOPHER SHINN

4.2

ELLEN: He just doesn't care—this job so obviously does not interest him—

JAQ: It's just amazing.

JAY: It's very upsetting—

ELLEN: The only response is to organize. Otherwise nothing will change—

(Gabe enters.)

Excuse me, Gabe?—If you have the President's ear I hope you'll use that access.

GABE: Anybody want to talk to these reporters who keep calling me? I really don't want to—

JAQ: Yes!

GABE: I'll message you their numbers.

(Gabe starts to go off. Jay follows him as Ellen and Jaq exit.)

JAY: Is everything okay?

GABE: Hey—sorry I've been out of touch. I've just been thinking a lot.

JAY: About what?

GABE: Just—the way people make themselves out to be such victims—I'm so over it. I wrote this long email to Drew asking
him for another chance—then I was like—he dumped me!

JAY: You didn't send it?

GABE: Nope. And, like, Tim talking constantly about wanting to
cheat on Jenny, like he *has to*—

JAY: Right—

GABE: Why can't people just stop being so self-pitying and so,
like, weak? I can't go out dancing one night without Drew—
and I invited him to come! I mean give me a *break*—

JAY: No, you behaved perfectly—

GABE: Tim's having a little rough patch in his relationship and
needs to *cheat*?

JAY: It's a lot of—very selfish, controlling behavior . . .

GABE: And I'm sorry, but I was nice to that kid. I spent three days
feeling guilty and bad and then I realized—I don't know what
was going on in that guy's head! No one does.

JAY: Uh-huh—

GABE: I reached out to him. I spoke to him at length—despite the
fact that he was pretty weird!

JAY: No, you shouldn't feel guilty—

GABE: This whole "blame the university" thing—it's so freaking
easy to do. Because then you can't blame the person who
actually chose to do what they did—another victim!

JAY: But—I mean, we don't know the whole story yet—but if that
really did happen to him—

GABE: If someone watched you with a guy on a webcam would you
kill yourself?

JAY: If I was closeted and worried it would get out—

GABE: He was out of the closet on his Facebook profile!

JAY: But that doesn't mean his parents knew—what if they were
really conservative—

GABE: Even so—you'd jump off the library balcony? I don't think
you would!

JAY: Not everyone's the same—maybe to him it was a really big
violation—

GABE: I'm not saying what happened had nothing to do with it,
just—this herd mentality—the vigils, the shrines, the status

updates—I just feel like no one is having an honest discussion about it. Everyone just wants him to be a total victim.

JAY: Well—I want to have an honest discussion about it. Do you want to get a drink later?

GABE: Yeah—I'd really like that.

JAY: Maybe go back to The Lair.

GABE: Oh yeah?

JAY: You still need to get me laid!

GABE: Ha, that's right. Okay—tonight then. *(Going)* Talk to you later, rollerblader!

JAY: Ha. Bye.

4.3

DREW: Come in.

(Nicky enters.)

What's up.

NICKY: I wanted to talk about the piece on Teddy—

DREW: I think it's great. We should get some more quotes from people who knew him in high school, but other than that—

NICKY: Right—well—I was doing some more research and—the piece is supposed to be a complete picture of who Teddy was, right?

DREW: Yeah?

NICKY: Well, it turns out that—he was on a message board on a porn site, and on a cam site—he didn't use his real name but there's overwhelming evidence, including pictures, that it's—

DREW: Uh-huh?

NICKY: It looks like he had a kind of—double life, pretending to be someone who's at the least a much cooler version of himself—online.

DREW: Does this add anything to the piece?

NICKY: Well yeah—it shows he might have been—not as timid as we've all been portraying him—he was an active player in these very exhibitionistic online worlds—

DREW: Has this been published anywhere else?

NICKY: Not yet, but if I can find all this stuff—it's just a matter of time.

(Pause.)

DREW: But I don't see what this has to do with his suicide.

NICKY: Well—everyone's talking about the rumors—people think he killed himself because he was exposed by his roommate. But at the same time he was exposing himself.

DREW: But that was his choice. It's not the same as being spied on—

NICKY: I agree—I just think it adds a level of complexity to him. And to the story.

DREW: But people will just use this to say that it can't be that he killed himself because his roommate live-streamed him. They'll use it to justify shifting blame away from—

NICKY: But this piece isn't about blame. It's just about who he actually was.

DREW: But that's what people will use it for. Also—it feels like another invasion of privacy.

NICKY: How?

DREW: You said he used a fake name. He meant this to be private. We'd be repeating—

NICKY: You didn't think it was an invasion of privacy when we outed Kevin Gillman.

(Pause.)

DREW: We didn't talk about his sex acts. We just said that he was—

NICKY: I don't have to be graphic. I can stick to the facts.

(Pause.)

DREW: Let me think about it, maybe it can be a separate story later on. Any roommate buzz?

NICKY: No one in the administration is talking. The investigations are ongoing—

DREW: Well get some more quotes from people he went to high school with—we have a lot from girls, see if there are any guys you can get quotes from.

NICKY: Okay.

(Pause.)

How are you doing post-breakup?

DREW: Fine.

NICKY: Gabe hasn't been in touch?

DREW: No—which is fine with me, I'm the one who ended it . . .

NICKY: Yeah . . . I hooked up with the hottest guy last night.

DREW: You did?

NICKY: After the vigil. He blew me in the parking lot. In between two cars.

DREW: Hot.

NICKY: It was such a good blowjob. Then he just got in his car and drove away.

DREW: You didn't reciprocate?

NICKY: Nah—wasn't in the mood.

DREW: Glad you got some action.

NICKY: Yeah . . . —Probably going out tonight if you want to come.

DREW: I don't go to gay bars. You know that.

NICKY: Just asking. All right.

(Nicky starts to go.)

DREW: Oh—I know I assigned you the candidates forum story— but I think I'm gonna take that myself, so you can just focus on the Teddy stuff.

NICKY: But—it won't take me that long to get a few—

DREW: I really want to do it.

NICKY: But . . . your ex-boyfriend is one of the candidates.

DREW: We dated for a week.

NICKY: Right . . .

(Pause.)

DREW: That's it—you can go.

4.4

TIM: "Part of what leadership is about is not just what you do, but the spirit with which you do it. I pledge to do my part to increase a spirit of friendliness on campus. If we are all a little nicer to one another, even just once or twice a day, we will see huge changes—"

JENNY: I think that part needs a little work.

TIM: Well—before when I talked about compassion and empathy you said I was too dramatic—

JENNY: But now it sounds like you're saying if everyone had been "a little nicer," Teddy—

TIM: —might not have killed himself—yeah.

JENNY: Sounds a little condescending. Don't be too dramatic, but don't underplay it either.

(Tim checks his phone.)

What?

TIM: Just—I don't understand why Gabe is not calling me back—

JENNY: I told you, he's probably just busy with Drew drama—

TIM: We talk every day—he has to be mad at me about something.

JENNY: You keep saying that—

TIM: If your best friend didn't call you for four days—

JENNY: But it's not like he's your boyfriend—

TIM: What do you mean?

JENNY: He doesn't have to call you back right away. He's a *friend*.

TIM: Not right away but . . .

JENNY: He's probably busy! Getting ready for tomorrow—

TIM: Too busy to text me and say sorry I haven't called?

JENNY: You are being such a girl!

TIM: Don't be mean.

JENNY: I'm not, I just don't understand why you're analyzing it so much!

TIM: We've talked or texted or emailed every day since freshman year—

JENNY: Well maybe it's time to grow out of that.

(Pause.)

What?

TIM: You're being really hurtful.

JENNY: Are you sure you're not in love with him?

TIM: Fuck you—

JENNY: I'm joking—

(Tim goes.)

4.5

GABE *(Coming over with shots)*: So anyone cruise you while I was at the bar?

JAY: Ummmm no.

GABE: Kinda slow night. But let's look around, there's gotta be someone here—

JAY: I think it must be that I smell or something.

GABE: You don't smell—

JAY: Just kidding.

GABE: Right— . . . —What about online? Have you tried to meet guys that way?

JAY: Most of the disabled guys out there seem to want able-bodied guys.

GABE: Really? Well—maybe this isn't at all what you want but—is it a fetish for some guys?

JAY: A few . . . but I don't want my body to be a metaphor for someone—like I'm "broken"—

GABE: Of course . . . Yeah, I dunno. Not looking very promising tonight, is it?

JAY: No . . .

There is *someone* here I like . . .

GABE: Oh yeah? Who?

(Pause. *Jay looks at Gabe. Gabe smiles and looks away. Nicky enters.*)

NICKY: Hey guys!

GABE: Oh—hey!

NICKY: What's up?

GABE: Just been—having shots, hanging out—

NICKY: Let me buy you another round—

GABE: Um—I don't know how—are you—

JAY: I'm up for another.

GABE: I—guess we'll have another round. We've been doing tequila shots so—

NICKY: Be right back!

(*Nicky goes. Pause.*)

GABE: He's sort of cute . . .

JAY: I guess. Not really my type.

GABE: Seeing him makes me think of Drew—which I'm trying not to do.

JAY: You want to go someplace else? Maybe just sit outside somewhere? It's so nice out.

GABE: Um . . . I don't know. —Probably better just to stay here for now.

JAY: Right.

I need to take a piss.

GABE: Okay . . .

(*Jay goes off. Nicky reenters.*)

NICKY: Is he leaving?

GABE: No, just going to the bathroom.

NICKY: That bathroom is bad enough when you can get in and out super fast—in a wheelchair—

GABE: I know. I don't know why they let it get so gross.

NICKY: Some guys are turned on by it.

GABE: I never understood how guys could have sex in bathrooms. Even "clean" ones—

NICKY: It's so gross. So—are you free?

GABE: Free?

NICKY: I mean, are you hanging with him all night or are you free to go as you please? It's gorgeous out—I thought you might like to take a walk.

GABE: A walk—that sounds very appealing . . .

NICKY: I mean it doesn't have to *just* be a walk . . .

GABE: Oh? We can run?

NICKY: Work up a sweat at least . . .

Not to be—I know it might be too early for you to—

GABE: I—it is kind of a—

NICKY: I really just wanna take a walk. Promise.

GABE: I . . . have this candidates' forum thing tomorrow—

NICKY: Not till ten.

GABE: Also, I feel bad just leaving my friend—

NICKY: We can walk him home.

GABE: Yeah? You wouldn't mind?

NICKY: Not at all.

(Jay enters.)

Your shot!

JAY: Thank you, good sir—

NICKY: Cheers, gentlemen!

(They drink.)

JAY: God—I need to take a bath in Purell after being in that bathroom.

NICKY: Yeah, we were just saying we're kind of over hanging out here.

GABE: We were—thinking about getting some fresh air, walking—walking around—do you want to stay here, or—we can walk with you back to your dorm . . .

JAY: Oh . . .

GABE: It's totally cool if you want to stay here—just thought if you weren't feeling it then . . .

JAY: Yeah—no, I think I'll just hang out here for a bit.

GABE: You sure?

JAY: Yeah. I can get myself home no problem.

GABE: Okay. So—

NICKY: Shall we?

GABE: Yeah—yeah. All right, so I'll talk to you soon.

JAY: Bye.

4.6

TIM: Hey, come in—

DREW: Thanks for seeing me so last-minute—

TIM: No problem—not doing anything except over-thinking tomorrow, so—

DREW: The more candidate interviews I do before the forum, the faster I can write the piece—

TIM: Cool—so—not many places to sit—you can take the chair— I'll sit on the bed I guess—

DREW: Whenever I'm in a dorm I feel like I've been magically transported to North Korea.

TIM: We can do it somewhere if that's easier—

DREW: Oh no, it'll only take ten minutes or so—I'll put my iPhone on your desk to record us—

TIM: You're lucky you got me, I was a couple stretches away from going out for a run—

DREW: I can see that—okay—I won't turn on the recorder yet so we can—ease into it.

    I feel a little—I know we both have Gabe in common . . . You probably know we broke—

TIM: Yeah—is that—still—

DREW: Yeah, it's over I think.

TIM: Sorry—

DREW: Thanks. You guys are really close, right?

TIM: Yeah—yeah we're . . .

DREW: Is it weird to be running against him? This is obviously off the—

TIM: Yeah—no, I mean—competition is a good thing.

DREW: Right, who has the bigger dick kind of thing—very male way of looking at it.

TIM: Well not who has the bigger—so much as—competition brings out the best in people.

DREW: Got it. —I was looking forward to meeting Jenny that night—sorry that didn't happen.

TIM: Well—she and I are fighting now so—who knows, we might breaking up, too—

DREW: What are you fighting about?

TIM: Honestly—I have no idea.

DREW: I feel like all fights between guys and girls on some level are about sex.

TIM: Really? How so?

DREW: I think deep down girls just know that guys have higher sex drives. Which means they must constantly be thinking about it . . . and that makes girls, like, insecure.

TIM: Huh.

DREW: I mean guys get off in a totally different kind of way—it's just like a physical release—whereas girls—

TIM: Makes sense—

DREW: Anyway—if I talk about sex it makes me want to have it so—I should get off the subject. Okay: let me get some background and then I'll turn on the—I'll tell you when I—

TIM: Okay—

DREW: So initially you weren't going to run—what changed your mind?

TIM: Just my love of serving.

DREW: Right . . . *Fuck.*

TIM: What?

DREW: Too late. Now I want to have sex.

    I thought I stopped myself in time . . . You're not hard, are you?

TIM: Me? No—

DREW: No, I was just curious. Sometimes talking about it . . .
　　　I am . . .

(Pause.)

　　　I won't tell anyone.

TIM: Tell anyone—what?

DREW: Oh—sorry. Just—seemed like you . . .
　　　I misunderstood. Sorry. I'll just go—

(Drew gets up, starts to go.)

TIM: You don't—I mean—you can't—it won't go away?

DREW: Does it ever go away for you?

TIM: Well . . . sometimes, yeah.

DREW: Like—after you rub one out—

TIM: No, like—I mean sometimes that but—if I think about some-
　　　thing not sex-related . . .

DREW: Yeah—that's not gonna work for me. You're a better man
　　　than I am.
　　　So . . .

TIM: If you—need to go . . .

DREW: I don't have to.

(Pause.)

TIM: Shit.
　　　Now I'm—

DREW: You're hard?

(Tim smiles. Drew goes over to him and touches him.)

　　　That's so hot . . .

TEDDY FERRARA

4.7

Gabe enters.

JAY: Hey!

GABE: Hi! I didn't know you were gonna be here.

JAY: I wouldn't miss it!

GABE: Thanks. —I'm so nervous about seeing Tim. I just texted him to say good luck . . .

JAY: That was really big of you.

GABE: How did your night end up?

JAY: The usual . . . Do you want to get lunch after this?

GABE: Um—I might be—Nicky and I might be grabbing a bite—

JAY: Oh—

GABE: He's actually here—just in the bathroom—

JAY: Wow. —Did you guys spend the night together?

GABE: We—nothing happened, we just snuggled. I don't know, we'll see—

JAY: That's great—

GABE: Yeah, I mean—it was just one—he told me some incredible stuff about Teddy Ferrara—

(Nicky enters.)

NICKY: Hey!
GABE: Hey—just chatting with—
JAY: Well I should get inside. Good luck.
GABE: Thanks!

(Jay wheels off.)

Think he's a little jealous that we . . . Anyway—I should probably—

(Drew enters.)

NICKY: Yeah, of course. I'll be cheering for you.
GABE: Thanks.

(Nicky leans in, kisses Gabe. Gabe goes off. Nicky starts off.)

DREW: Nicky.
NICKY: Oh—hey—
DREW: What are you doing here?
NICKY: Oh—just—going in to watch—
DREW: You're watching the forum?
NICKY: Gabe wanted me to come.
DREW: How are you doing on those quotes?
NICKY: I—have calls in—nobody's called me back yet—
DREW: Okay. Oh—wanted to tell you—someone published the webcam stuff about Teddy.
NICKY: They did?
DREW: Some hipster media blog. The story's out there now so—no need for us to do it.
NICKY: What—was the gist of the—
DREW: I'll send you the link. Has a kind of trashy feel. Reader feedback is really negative.

(Tim enters.)

So—just focus on getting those quotes so we can get the profile in tomorrow's paper.

NICKY: Okay.

DREW: We need them ASAP—I'd get on the phone again now.

NICKY: I'll do it after the—

DREW: Text him, he'll understand—I really need that story.

NICKY: They'll call me back when they—

DREW: I need the story now!

(Pause. Nicky goes. Tim walks past Drew.)

Hey Tim—

(Tim ignores Drew and keeps walking off.)

4.8

TIM *(Entering)*: Hey.

GABE: Oh—hey.

TIM: Do you know the story?

GABE: I think the President is going to make remarks and then—
I'm not sure the order but—

TIM: Cool.

(Pause.)

GABE: Did you get my text?

TIM: I did, yeah.
I'm gonna go practice my—

GABE: Okay . . .

4.9

PRESIDENT: . . . and it's in that spirit that I'm here—the Provost is here—I see a lot of faculty—and all of you guys—this is a real example of what can happen at a university—people getting together from all different communities—and talking and listening to one another.

Now after all the candidates for the different offices have given their five-minute statements—they'll come onstage for a Q&A. I believe we're starting with the candidates for President—our first—is that Gabe? I don't have, no one gave me the order . . .

(Gabe enters. President exits.)

GABE *(Over microphone)*: Thank you. I'm running for Student Assembly President because I want to make specific, concrete changes to university life. I'm not here to speak in platitudes or abstractions—

JAQ'S VOICE *(Through megaphone)*: No more silence, no more hate—time for us to demonstrate!

GABE: Um—

JAQ *(Entering; through megaphone)*: No more silence, no more hate—time for us to demonstrate!

(President enters, takes mike from Gabe.)

PRESIDENT: Now this is a good example of something you have a *right* to do—but is *not right* to—

JAQ: Teddy Ferrara is dead! Say something about that!

PRESIDENT: You know that we are all thinking deeply about what—

JAQ: NO MORE SILENCE—NO MORE HATE—TIME FOR US TO DEMONSTRATE!

PRESIDENT: You're *loud,* but is anyone *hearing* you—ask yourself that—

JAQ: Ask yourself to look in the mirror!

PRESIDENT: I'll put down the mike if you put down the megaphone—we can have a discussion later—

JAQ: Later? Later? There is no later for Teddy Ferrara—

PRESIDENT: This is a forum for candidates for Student Assembly to address the issues facing—

JAQ: TO PAD THEIR RÉSUMÉS—TO SUCK UP TO POWER—

PRESIDENT: You don't have career ambitions? I just saw you on TV—

GABE: I wouldn't—

JAQ *(Joined by offstage voices)*: NO MORE SILENCE—NO MORE HATE—TIME FOR US TO—

PRESIDENT: So this was a big thing, all planned out—

JAQ *(With voices)*: DEMONSTRATE! DEMONSTRATE! DEMON-STRATE! DEMONSTRATE—

PRESIDENT *(Reaching for megaphone)*: Can security—can we take that—do we not have a policy about—

(He tries to grab the megaphone. Jaq resists.)

GABE: I wouldn't—just—

PRESIDENT: This is a *candidate's forum*—

(President rips the megaphone from Jaq.)

JAQ: My God, he's assaulting me! He's assaulting me, was that recorded—

PRESIDENT: No, I'm trying to engage you in conversation, which is what you claim to want—

JAQ: By grabbing me—we have that on film—

PRESIDENT: Fine—you know what else you have? A canceled event—

(President throws down the megaphone and exits. Jaq retrieves it.)

JAQ: SPEAK FOR TEDDY! SHOUT FOR TEDDY! CRY FOR TEDDY! FIGHT FOR TEDDY! HIS VOICE IS OURS—OUR VOICE IS HIS! HIS VOICE IS OURS—OUR VOICE IS HIS!

(Gabe exits.)

4.10

PRESIDENT: Did you see that?

PROVOST: Security is coming.

PRESIDENT: Why aren't they here?

PROVOST: There was one guy in the auditorium—he radioed—he
wasn't clear about the policy—

PRESIDENT: These kids are fucking infants!

PROVOST: I'd keep it down—I'm sure everyone has their phones
out—

PRESIDENT: I don't care, let them record me—assault?!

PROVOST: It didn't look good when you tried to take the—

PRESIDENT *(Going)*: I don't give a fuck—I just got elected to the
Senate. Fuck this place.

(Provost follows President off.
Sounds of protest from off. Drew enters. Gabe comes out. He
sees Drew.)

GABE: Hey.

DREW: Could you believe that?

GABE: Crazy.

DREW: I know. Are you okay?

GABE: Yeah—I was just like—what do I—

DREW: You did exactly the right thing—tried to keep everyone calm—didn't overreact—

GABE: I didn't know what else to—

DREW: You were amazing.

(Pause.)

GABE: Thank you . . .

5.1

Drew enters.

DREW: What's up?

NICKY: Hey.

DREW: Why didn't you want to come to the office?

NICKY: Because . . . I wanted to talk to you on more neutral ground.

DREW: I guess we'll get to why—can't get more neutral than the food court. What's up?

NICKY: Now that charges have come down in Teddy's case—I feel like the story is basically over.

DREW: There's no hate crime charge yet. That's a story—that they just went with invasion of—

NICKY: I mean—he's dead, the roommate left school, the charges are filed, the university is having this big event tomorrow before the Homecoming game—I'd like to move on.

DREW: Well . . . okay. You've done a great job but we can find you other stuff to cover—

NICKY: No, I mean—I'd like to move on from the paper.

(Pause.)

DREW: Why?

NICKY: I'm burned-out. On top of all my schoolwork it's just too much.

DREW: All of a sudden?

NICKY: It's been building . . .

DREW: Right. Are you sure this isn't about something else?

NICKY: No—no.

DREW: Are you mad that Gabe and I got back together?

(Pause.)

NICKY: Why would that make me mad? We had one—

DREW: Because you're in love with me?

NICKY: Drew—that's ridiculous.
　　I'm not in love with you.

(Pause.)

DREW: Okay. Just—okay.

NICKY: What?

DREW: No, just . . . guess I misread you. I thought you were flirting with me . . .

NICKY: I mean—I was but—so were you.

DREW: Oh, I know I flirted with you. For sure.

(Pause.)

NICKY: So why did you never . . . pursue anything?

DREW: I wanted to. I just didn't think it was ethical. You worked for me.

(Pause.)

NICKY: I don't anymore.

DREW: Right—but I'm with Gabe now. So . . .

NICKY: . . . That's how it goes I guess.

DREW: Well. I hate to lose a great writer, but— Are you still going to read your piece in the—

NICKY: Yeah, I'll still take part in the ceremony—

CHRISTOPHER SHINN

106

DREW: Okay. Doing anything for Homecoming kickoff tonight?

NICKY: Probably just catch up with schoolwork.

DREW: Nothing? Not even going to see *Beach Crew*?

NICKY: Oh God no—

DREW: Can I ask you one question? Will you promise to be honest?

NICKY: Sure.

DREW: When you told me that after the vigil some guy blew you— were you lying?

NICKY: No. Why?

DREW: Really?

(Pause.)

NICKY: I'm not—

DREW: Just tell me the truth.

(Pause.)

NICKY: No, I wasn't lying.

DREW: Okay.
I gotta get back to work—I'll see you at the ceremony tomorrow.

NICKY: You'll be there?

DREW: Gabe has to be there as head of the Queer Students, so— I'm going for him.

5.2

GABE: Wow. I wonder if what happened had anything to do with his deciding to declare?

JAY: He was so clearly acting out. It was like he wanted an excuse—

GABE *(Reading on phone)*: ". . . nothing to do with real or perceived tensions at the university"—

JAY: Liar—which makes him perfect for the Senate!

GABE: I guess he has to say that. It's too bad—I think he was a good President.

JAY: You do? Really? I know you liked him as a person but—how was he a good—

GABE: He's an adult. And he expected everyone here to also be an adult—

JAY: Violently ripping a megaphone from a student is adult behavior?

GABE: In context—sure.

JAY: I think an adult would have allowed an act of protest to unfold.

GABE: In the middle of my speech?

JAY: I wish they'd waited but—it had to be at a moment when it would make an impact.

GABE: Right . . . —Hopefully I can work on his campaign. How amazing would that be.

JAY: If that's the kind of thing you want to do . . .

GABE: You know, some good things do happen in Congress—Americans with Disabilities Act?

JAY: You don't have to lecture me on the Americans with Disabilities—

GABE: No I wasn't—lecturing—

JAY: A lot of very bad things happen there, too.

(Pause.)

GABE: Well—I like him. And I think his caution proved correct—when the real story came out—

JAY: Not this again—

GABE: But the reason we have to be careful with grand pronouncements is they oversimplify—

JAY: There's a reason no legitimate news outlets ever reported that stuff—

GABE: Yeah, because they want everything to be black and white—

JAY: No, because it had nothing to do with Teddy killing himself—

GABE: Nobody can say why he killed himself—

JAY: You just refuse to even consider the possibility it was the obvious reason, though. Why?

GABE: I don't—I just don't think we can know either way . . .
    Anyway. You doing anything tonight?

JAY: I'm not sure yet.

GABE: Me and Drew are getting together with Tim and Jenny if you want to join us.

JAY: You patched things up with Tim?

GABE: He did! I don't know how he heard so quickly that Drew and I got back together—but he texted me this morning and asked if we wanted to get drinks.

JAY: That's it? You never talked about the fact that you stopped being in touch with him?

GABE: I thought more about it—I think I overreacted—I was stressed about Drew at the time . . .

JAY: I remember you being really upset that he kept saying he was going to cheat.

GABE: But he didn't actually do it—

JAY: What do you like about Drew? I don't really understand.

(Pause.)

GABE: I just—like him—his energy, his spirit, his drive—

JAY: Do you respect him?

GABE: I do. He's overcome a lot of hurt—his parents—there was a guy who really hurt him—

JAY: I've overcome a lot of hurt.

(Pause.)

I have a good spirit and drive. And I actually care about you.

GABE: I—Drew cares about me . . .

(Pause.)

JAY: You can't even acknowledge what I'm saying.

GABE: I—what do you want me to say? You have great qualities but—you're in a wheelchair.

(Pause.)

JAY: Thank you for saying that.

I don't think I'm going to go out with you guys tonight.

GABE: Okay. —Why not?

JAY: I don't respect those people.

GABE: You're being an asshole.

JAY: Right. I'm the asshole—

(Gabe goes.)

CHRISTOPHER SHINN

5.3

JENNY: What do we have left to toast to?

TIM: Remind me again? We toasted to not being at the *Beach Crew* show tonight—

DREW: To senior year—

TIM: To winning the football game—

GABE: Ugh, I can't believe we wasted a toast on that—

JENNY: What's left?

GABE: We also toasted to not having jobs when we graduate—

TIM: Right, blocked that one out—

DREW: I know!

JENNY: What?

DREW: To the best man winning on Monday.

TIM: Good one! To the election!

JENNY: Cheers!

GABE: Cheers—

TIM: But we know who's gonna win.

GABE: We do?

TIM: Not to be insensitive but—since the gay kid died—the gay guy's gonna win. Done deal.

GABE: You don't know that—

JENNY: Speaking of which—we haven't talked about the charges against the roommate!

DREW: Yeah—no hate crime charge, at least not yet—

TIM: I had people in my Civil Rights class saying it should be manslaughter!

GABE: That's insane—in a *suicide* case?

JENNY: I don't want to sound like a nazi but—did the kid really do anything *that* wrong?

TIM: You could definitely argue that it falls within typical collegiate behavior—

JENNY: I mean this kid's gonna go to *jail*? What's the maximum—

DREW: Five years—

JENNY: The kid's a jerk but—

GABE: Well you better believe that all that stuff about Teddy is gonna come out at trial—

TIM: Right, all the stuff the newspapers wouldn't print—

GABE: I mean the roommate obviously at the least made a mistake and was a jerk—

DREW: Harassed, bullied, intimidated, spied—

TIM: Typical Saturday night at a frat—

DREW: But he didn't join a frat—he had an expectation of—

TIM: No, true—I don't think we should underplay it. He broke a law—

JENNY: But the defense is gonna be that the roommate was nervous about who Teddy was bringing over—he just wanted to see what the guy was like—

GABE: *That's* hard to believe—

TIM: It's at least a little believable—that dude was kind of weird, you'd want to know who—

JENNY: And I hear the guy was sketchy—some people said he looked homeless or something—

GABE: But there's all the roommate's homophobic Facebook and Twitter posts—

DREW: Right—the "curious to see who it was" defense won't work—

TIM: There's all the hype now but—I bet the kid makes a plea—no jail time—

JENNY: Nobody's said the obvious thing though, about why he might have done it—

GABE: What?

JENNY: Maybe he was gay! Like—he wanted to watch—

DREW: I don't think so—he watched from a girl's room, seems like—

JENNY: Yeah, which is what you would do if you wanted to cover up—

TIM: If he wanted to watch a guy—no offense but—I don't think that's the guy you'd—

JENNY: But being homophobic is a sign of being gay, right? Ooh we could ask Tim—the expert—

TIM: Ha—yeah—

JENNY: He thought he could tell for sure that Kevin Gillman wasn't gay—

TIM: I—no, not that I knew—

JENNY: You were pretty confident—

TIM: I'm gonna take a piss. By the time I get back hopefully we'll have exhausted this topic!

GABE: Don't take too long or you'll get accused of being gay!

TIM: Ha!

(Tim goes.)

JENNY: I think we need more shots!

GABE: We do *not.*

JENNY: I'll take that as a yes!

(Jenny goes.)

GABE: We are not having those shots. And neither should they—

DREW: Why not?

GABE: We all have to be at this event in the morning—

DREW: Teddy totally took the spotlight off Kevin. No one's talking about him—pisses me off.

(Pause.)

GABE: Yeah, but . . . Kevin—was last year—

DREW: The whole point of that article was to raise awareness about guys who are in the closet, who are passing as straight—and now everyone's just focused on this gay geek—

GABE: Whoa—

DREW: It's almost like he was jealous. Like he read the article and wanted to upstage Kevin.

GABE: Drew—that's crazy.

DREW: It's not—a lot of these little loser gay guys can't deal with the fact that hotter and straighter-acting guys are starting to come out of the closet. The world is changing. Being gay is not just some silly little effeminate, queer, faggoty thing anymore—

GABE: Where are you—seeing all these supposedly straight-acting gay guys?—

DREW: We're both pretty straight-acting.

GABE: We're not *flaming*—but I don't think we seem *straight*—

DREW: If I walk down the street people don't *know*.

GABE: I—wouldn't be so sure of that.

DREW: Um—that's why straight guys are attracted to me. I seem like them.

GABE: Wait—straight guys are *attracted* to you?

DREW: Whether they're straight or not—I can't say but—a certain kind of guy, yeah.

GABE: What are you—who?

DREW: Well—Tim finds me attractive.

GABE: Tim?

DREW: Yeah. We hooked up, actually.

(Pause.)

GABE: What?

DREW: The other night. It was before we got back together—

GABE: Wait—are you kidding?

DREW: No. We messed around.

I'm sorry if it upsets you—you said you weren't attracted to him so I thought . . . I didn't know we were gonna get back together—

GABE: When . . .

DREW: I was interviewing him and . . .

It just sort of happened.

(Pause.
Tim enters.)

TIM: All right—what are we talking about? Don't disappoint me!

DREW: Ha—

TIM: I can't believe how early it is. How are we this drunk this early?

GABE: Yeah, we should probably—

(Jenny returns with shots.)

JENNY *(Toasting)*: To getting FUCKED UP!

TIM: I think that's all we have left—

(All save Gabe drink.)

Dude!

(Pause. Gabe drinks.)

Phew. Close one!

JENNY: Remind me to start drinking a lot of water an hour ago.

DREW: Just got a text—a lot more people showed up to that *Beach Crew* show than have tickets—

TIM: God bless America—

GABE: Guys—I feel sick, I think I need to go home.

TIM: Oh no!

JENNY: You okay—want us to walk you?

GABE: No, I'm fine—

DREW: I'll go with you—

GABE: I'd rather be alone—I just—it'll help me clear my head—

TIM: You sure you're okay?

GABE: I'll be fine—

(Gabe goes.)

TIM: Was that weird?

DREW: That's Gabe, though. He overthinks things. He probably has a headache that he's misinterpreting as an existential crisis.

JENNY: I can see that.

TIM: I hope he's okay—

DREW: Trust me, he'll be fine.

5.4

GABE *(On phone)*: Hey Jay . . . hard to imagine you're asleep so I guess you're just not picking up—I'm—outside the—auditorium—the *Beach Crew* show is about to let out I think—

I'm—not doing so well tonight. Which can you probably tell. So—if you can, call me . . .

(Ends call. Pause. Dials.)

Nicky. Hey. So. You probably maybe don't want to hear from me . . . buuuuut in case you—do—if you happen to be in the *Beach Crew* show—I'm just outside—maybe you wanna—take a walk or . . .

Fuck it. Erase.

5.5

NICKY: He's so fucking shallow. I'm sorry—I know I keep saying that—

JAY: No—I don't know him, but from what I've heard—

NICKY: And he gets everything. Why? Why does everyone want him so much?

JAY: Oh look—I have another message from Gabe. Wonder what this one says.

NICKY: Whatever happened—I'm sure he'll go running back to him tomorrow.

(Jay listens. Nicky checks his phone.)

JAY: Yeah, same. Boo-hoo.
    Who called?

NICKY: Gabe—but of course he didn't leave a message. You're not calling him back so he's moving down his list of people to cry about Drew to.

JAY: Unbelievable.

NICKY: Whatever.
    All right. It's not happening here for me.

JAY: No . . .

We could go somewhere and get something to eat?

(Pause.)

NICKY: I think I'm gonna call it a night. Go to bed early.
JAY: Okay . . .
NICKY: Have a good one.
JAY: Bye.

5.6

Library balcony. Gabe looks at a book. Pause. He goes to restroom and enters.

Inside the bathroom. Gabe enters a stall. He closes the door. He sits, fully clothed.

Nicky enters. Bends down, checks stalls. Goes into the next stall. Shuts door. Sits. Gabe moves his foot over a bit. Nicky mirrors him. Their sneakers touch.

GABE *(Whispers)*: Hey.

> *(Nicky extends his hand below the stall wall, motions with it. Gabe kneels down and positions his pelvis below the stall wall. He unzips.)*

You want that?

> *(Nicky reaches inside Gabe's pants. Campus Police enter quietly. They look under the stall doors.)*

POLICE 1 *(Loudly)*: Come out of the stalls now—

POLICE 2: Come out of there.

(Gabe quickly zips up. Nicky opens the door and steps out.)

NICKY: What is this about—

(Gabe opens the door and steps out.)

GABE: What's going on—
POLICE 1: Come with us—

(Gabe and Nicky see each other.)

GABE: I didn't—we weren't doing anything—
POLICE 2: Follow us, and you can explain whatever—
GABE: We weren't—I don't understand what's—
POLICE 1: Are you going to comply?
NICKY: Yes.
GABE: No—no—nothing—
POLICE 2: Let's go—
GABE: Nothing was—
POLICE 2: Now.

5.7

PRESIDENT: I want first of all to say that it's wonderful to be here with this diverse group behind me: my good friend and colleague—Ellen; two inspiring young people I've gotten to know during a series of conversations about GLBTQ issues—Jay, Jaq; outgoing (possibly incoming) Student Assembly President—Tim; and the fearless editor of the *Daily*—Drew; thank you all for being here.

It's truly a wonderful group. I think all of us would agree— we would all feel *similarly* that *difference* is so important to the life of a university—and to the world. And that if we can—learn to accept difference—something that people who are different have had to do, often from a very early age—but if those of us who haven't had to learn to accept difference so much—because of the race or class or gender or sexual orientation we were born into—if we can learn to accept difference, we will one day have the kind of world that will feel like home to everyone.

Before I say a few words about the extraordinary young man we're here today to honor—Teddy Ferrara—and the new facility that will bear his name—I've asked Drew to read a small section of an extraordinary profile of Teddy that the *Daily* published. Drew?

(Drew comes forward.)

DREW: Thank you. This is from the end of the piece . . . "Ultimately, those who knew Teddy best say that what was lost is not just someone whose future was bright and who had much to offer to the world. What was lost is someone whose kindness and gentleness were rare in this world, whose essentially caring nature was the exception and not the rule."

(Tim exits.)

"Teddy Ferrara was not someone who was loud and aggressive, clamoring for attention and popularity. He was a sweet soul, seeking love and light in an all too-dark world."

5.8

JENNY *(Following after Tim)*: What's wrong?

TIM: I feel sick.

JENNY: Gabe will be fine—

TIM: I just got—

JENNY: Like you said—they didn't press criminal charges, he'll probably just go on probation—

TIM: I got a text—there's a story on the *Daily* website—

JENNY: Who texted you?—

TIM: There's an article about what happened in the library—it just went up—

JENNY: Oh—

TIM: For the rest of his life it'll be on the internet—so when he applies for a job or—

JENNY: Well—it's not your fault—

TIM: I just . . .

Why would he do this? *Why?*

JENNY: Who knows? You can't know . . .

Let's go back to the ceremony—

TIM: I don't think I can.

JENNY: You have to. The President just introduced you—

TIM: I . . .

JENNY: Tim—the whole state is watching this.

(Pause.)

TIM: Right . . .

JENNY: You can do it.

(Pause.)

Ready?

(Pause. Tim takes Jenny's hand. They walk off together.)

END OF PLAY

CHRISTOPHER SHINN is the author of *Dying City* (Pulitzer Prize finalist), *Now or Later* (Evening Standard Theatre Award for Best Play shortlist), *Where Do We Live* (Obie Award for Playwriting) and *Four*. He teaches playwriting at the New School for Drama.